BOATS and BOATMEN of PAKISTAN

Here, in one street, were the people who made sail cloth for the ships; and at the foot of it were shipyards, where shipwrights and carpenters were building the ships of wood; and there is immense interest and education in watching a boat being built

T. R. Glover *The Ancient World*

BY THE SAME AUTHOR

The Merchant Schooners, Volumes 1 & 2
Sailing for a Living

EDITED & PREFACED

Out of Appledore by W. J. Slade

PAMPHLETS

Concise Guide to the National Maritime Museum
The Boats of East Pakistan
The Great Migration
Nonsuch
Captain Cook

WITH ANN GIFFARD

Westcountrymen in Prince Edward's Isle
The Merchant Sailing Ship: A Photographic History
Women Under Sail

A deep-laden *ghashi* sailing in a winter breeze

BOATS and BOATMEN of PAKISTAN

Basil Greenhill

Foreword by Alan Villiers

DAVID & CHARLES · NEWTON ABBOT

ISBN 0 7153 5009 9

Set in eleven on thirteen point Garamond
and printed in Great Britain
by Bristol Typesetting Company Limited
for David & Charles (Publishers) Limited
South Devon House Newton Abbot Devon

Again in memory of Gillian, who shared all the travels which gave rise to this book and then died of amoebic hepatitis picked up somewhere in East Pakistan

CONTENTS

ILLUSTRATIONS

PLATES

DRAWINGS IN THE TEXT

MAPS

FOREWORD

I have been delighted to read this book, a most excellent and long overdue study in a rich and fascinating field. I have some slight acquaintance with the area myself from a visit there in 1956 (my interest aroused by Basil Greenhill, well known to me through our joint association over the years with the Society for Nautical Research). I had three main interests in Indian waters about that time—to learn about the classic big *dhows* then still operating out of the ancient ports of the long-established Portuguese enclaves of Goa, Damao, and Diu; to sail with the islanders of the Maldives in their last brig, if I could find her, between Ceylon and Male in the Maldive Islands; and to have a good look at, and sail with, the fleets of the Sundarbans, of Chittagong and the Karnafuli, above all of the vast river complex called Brahmaputra. I was late, even in '56. I had to fly to Goa from Karachi over the sea, by small four-engined De Havilland aircraft, to find the big dhows—or a few of them—still there, but blockaded in port. All that sailed were local craft ferrying iron ore to the steamers at Mormagoa. The Sultan of the Maldives still had a small fleet of large Indian-built *baggalas*, but when I reached his capital of Male in one of these from Colombo it was to find the last brig anchored in the lagoon, rigged down and being broken up, though she looked as good as new and her lines were beautiful. Poor brig! The Majlis wanted a motor-ship as fit for the modern image, and they had landing rights at Addu Atoll to trade for her.

I did better at Calcutta, for I found passage—thanks to the Joint Steamer Company, a friendly and efficient concern—by the interesting side-wheeler *Shwebo* towards Gauhati in Assam by way of the Sundarbans and sundry arms of the Brahmaputra system. Gone were the tea-planters, the crowds of passengers deck and cabin: it was a time of some tension between India and Pakistan and the Brahmaputra under some name or other wound its busy way across the border far too often. Each crossing meant delay, bother with documents. It was all very well while I was in the *Shewbo*, but I wondered how I might get on if I were sailing in local craft.

These we saw in splendid profusion and great diversity, sailing gracefully under their widespread square sails which, when a fleet was approaching, looked exactly as if some forgotten fleet of galleons had somehow suddenly been conjured from the mists of the river and brought to a glorious and astonishing life. To be sure, close view dispelled the illusion, for they were rigged for assured perfection of weather and fair winds, and the greater part of the hull was taken up by a large thatched house—cargo cover and crew accommodation combined. But often I saw more square sails pass me in a sunlit morning than had passed the Horn during the previous quarter-century. How beautiful they all were! Points of grace in hull were obvious at close quarters, as they sailed down or poled, paddled, or towed upstream.

The *Shwebo* got me, in time, to Gauhati: in due course I went on by smaller steamer to Jorhat, and thence to Dibrugarh, which was about as far as one could use the river then in Upper Assam. There was trouble with hill tribes towards the Burma border: there were difficulties with infiltrating Chinese. And an earthquake had raised the bed of the river at and beyond Dibrugarh. These were hard times for the wandering student, just interested in ships and seaman, craft and craftsmen. I managed, in due course, to spend fascinating time at Dacca, Khulna, Chittagong. I saw a lot, learned a little. But what about this idea of sailing in the craft and getting down to bedrock with the subject? I'd been able to do that with the Kuwaiti and the Yemenites: but that was pre-war, and they were deepwatermen. Even so, it had taken a good three months to become acclimatised: I had had dysentery, malaria, and so forth.

I observed that the Brahmaputra river-men drank the river water. They were among millions who used it also for every other purpose known to man. Long usage gave them immunity, I hoped, for there was cholera about. More germs to the gallon lurked in that brown water than enough: and I had no immunity at all. The Kuwaiti and the Yemenites had at least had access to mosque wells. And the upset political conditions in newly independent countries are not helpful to peaceful travellers: an interest in ships and seamen could be looked upon as so astonishing as to merit disbelief. What was I really up to? There are some risks, I concluded, that it is foolish to take. Though I was aware that until then at any rate, no one had taken real time out to study this immense, diverse, unspoiled and fascinating shipping, it could not then be for me. I picked up a little fever. I hoped that before long, someone would take up the subject.

I need not have worried. Even then Basil Greenhill was devoting leaves and spare time to learning all he could. A westcountryman by birth, long interested and knowledgeable in the ways of ships and the sea, his knowledge and his curiosity extended to craft, boats, and rivers too. A long-standing member and Councillor of the Society for Nautical Research, he believed in practical personal investigation of the material at hand, as I did. When this was the way to learn things, he got on with it.

He got on with it indeed, in those more interesting history and craft-rich waters. There could not have been a better man. The results are in the fascinating story here presented.

Oxford, 1970

Alan Villiers

Part 1

THE MONSOON COUNTRY

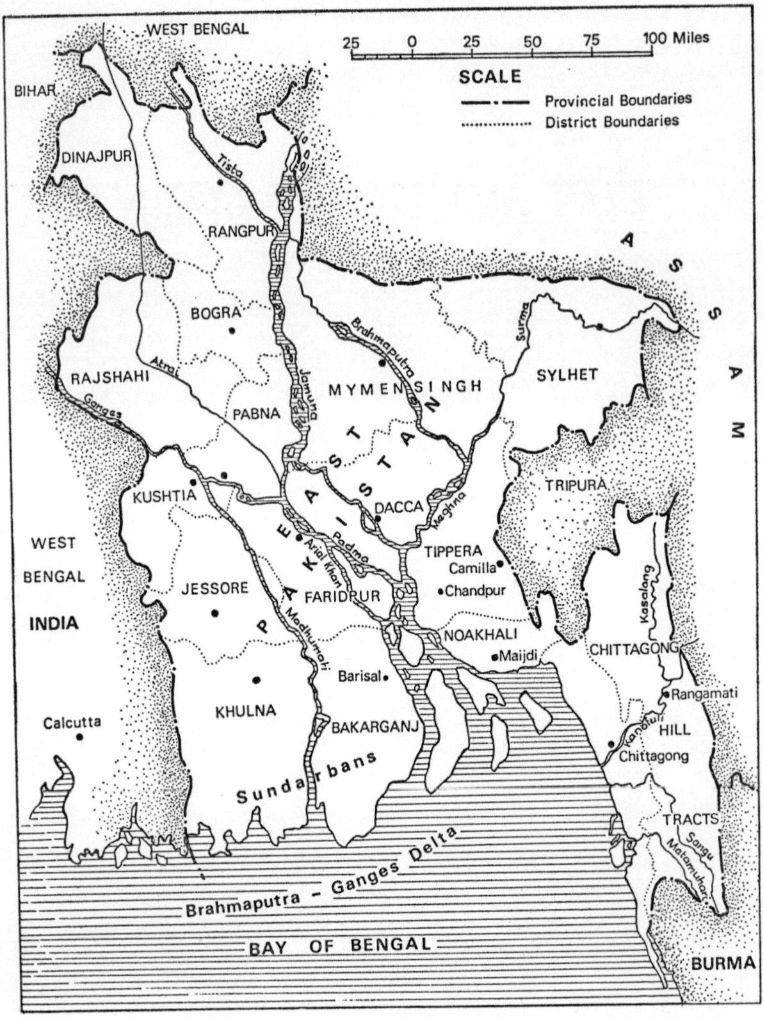

East Pakistan

One

THE BIG RIVERS

East Pakistan has a climate in which occur extremes of annual rainfall, of humidity combined with relatively high temperatures and of winds. Local thunderstorms with very high wind speeds occur in April and May, more widespread cyclones as violent as the hurricanes of Eastern North America, but even more devastating because the land lies just above sea level and there is no escape from the exceptional and sudden tides which accompany these storms, happen almost every year, most recent and disastrously in November, 1970, when early reports suggest that 100,000 people may have died. The chapters which follow in the first part of this book describe the way of life of the people, and especially of that large part of them who are boatmen, of this land of natural violence.

In this book I have recorded some of the facts about boats and boatmen in both provinces of Pakistan as I saw them in five years of living in the country. The first part of the book deals with the East, the second with the boats and boatmen of the West.

There are still relatively few signs that the great mass of the boats of East Pakistan have been affected by recent technological developments elsewhere in the world. The existence of the boats and of the living the boatmen can earn with them depends, of course, on the developed world's demand for the raw materials they carry, and there are more and probably bigger boats than there would be if the country did not grow most of the world's jute. But nothing in their fabric depends on anything that cannot be made by carpenter, blacksmith and village weaver. If all the world's sources of power were to dry up tomorrow the boats of

East Pakistan could be built just as they were before, even though some of them are very sophisticated boats of their kind.

Arab seafarers came to East Pakistan (Map 1) more than a thousand years ago in search of trade, or kingdoms, and to spread Islam. They settled in Chittagong to the south and they sailed up the eastern rivers into the districts nowadays called Noakhali and Tipperah and Sylhet and they peopled the southern islands of the estuary, Sandwip and Hatiya. Everywhere they went they left a legacy of Arab words in the local dialect, and of sharp featured strong looking people who are great watermen, and outward looking and adventurous. Later these people made up perhaps half the Asian crews of British deep sea ships.

After the Arabs came the Afghans from the central Asian upland, who conquered Delhi and set up a kingdom on the banks of the great rivers roughly about the time the Crusaders were worrying at the flanks of the Arab civilisation in the Middle East. Then came the Portuguese in search of fine fabrics and rice, the Dutch and the French and the Moghul conquerors from the banks of the Oxus, who set up a stable government, for a while.

Finally the British established themselves and made their capital at Calcutta, away to the west beyond the rivers, at the edge of the high land. Then the river country became a source of raw materials, a sort of kitchen garden of eastern India, where indigo and rice and later jute and tea were cultivated to be consumed elsewhere. Paddle steamers now explored the river routes, some railways were built, but no roads, and Calcutta grew and grew until with nearly 3 million people packed into its miles of slums it became the second city of the Empire.

In 1905 there was a reorganisation of government and the eastern region became part of a province on its own with its own capital, the old Moghul city of Dacca. For political reasons this land of rivers lost its status as a separate province after a few years. But when the cry for a separate Muslim homeland in the Indian sub-continent was heard in the early 1940s, the eastern part of Bengal was claimed as part of it, and in 1947, when independent India and Pakistan were created, it became East Pakistan.

The Brahmaputra, under its various names in what is now East Pakistan, nearly bisects a land of 42 million people packed into 54,000 square miles, a country with more than half the population of the world's largest Muslim state. It is a great plain, ringed with hills and jungles, shattered over much of its area into thousands of fragments by the great rivers, dotted with mounds raised above the flood level and covered with trees and houses. Much of the land in between these mounds passes many feet under water for six months of the year during and after the south-west monsoon. So its people are a nation of boatmen.

The rivers form what is perhaps the most complete system of inland navigation to be found anywhere in the world. The early European navigators and seamen were completely bewildered by their complexity—it was two hundred years before their courses were mapped at all accurately—and delighted by the relatively easy road they gave to the interior of the country. The quick establishment of British control over Bengal was due partly to the fact that travel was comparatively easy and comparatively large quantities of trade goods could be moved to and from the interior. In 1781 Rennell, British Surveyor General of Bengal and sometimes called the father of Indian geography, estimated that this inland trade gave employment to at least 30,000 boatmen. Today the population has increased at least fivefold and trade very much more, so that 1 million is probably a nearer estimate of the number of professional boatmen on these rivers.

The pattern of waterways that faced the first Portuguese, French and British explorers and traders and adventurers was not the same as the pattern of waterways the boatmen know today. For the rivers are always changing. An unending cycle of land building goes on all the time. Gradually the main courses of the rivers have shifted, generally eastwards across towards the mountains of Assam. Every stream flowing through the area deposits silt, builds up its own bed, overflows, and finds a new course, perhaps washing away some old high ground and depositing it somewhere else in the process. But sometimes changes are dramatic, as when in 1787 the river Teesta in the northern part of the country flooded and changed its course to a new junction with the great Brahmaputra. And then the Brahmaputra itself changed its course, abandoning the busy town of Mymensingh to rural solitude, and found a new channel due south to join the Ganges.

These great changes in the rivers make the local history of the country difficult to follow, because the highroads of today are the backwaters of tomorrow, the river bed of today the solid land of two generations ago. Dacca, the capital of East Pakistan, was founded by the Moghuls probably at a point where the great river Ganges washed the southernmost tip of the long triangle of high, jungle covered land which stretches from the Garo Hills in Assam and is always above even the highest floods. The Ganges flowed on to join the Brahmaputra somewhere to the south-east. Today they join far to the north-west of Dacca and the city stands on a shallow backwater, the Burri Ganga, an offshoot of an offshoot of the big rivers.

The great Brahmaputra is always changing its course a little, this way and that, it never runs exactly the same place for two successive years. No permanent buildings can be put up on its banks. The terminal points of ferries, the ends of roads and railways, can never be fixed. The railway track at Goalundo, the terminus of the main railway line from Dacca to Calcutta, has to be relaid every year. In the dry season it leads over an arid desert of silt to the water's edge. Even then the whole place is unstable. I remember once lying all night in a steamer off Goalundo and in the early morning there was a roar and a series of great waves as fifteen or twenty feet of the river bank peeled off into the water. In the next monsoon the whole place was swept away and the site of Goalundo moved miles to the west. On the other hand, what were marshy islets when the British first surveyed Bengal are now densely populated areas. In places, it is said, the land has recently advanced into the Bay of Bengal at the rate of half a mile a year.

The peculiar character of this monsoon country of East Pakistan and, in particular, the parts of it which are subject to annual inundation can best be pictured in terms of everyday experience.

Shortly after we first arrived in Dacca we drove out along what was then a brick surfaced road as far as the bridge over the Burri Ganga river at Mirpur, where the river curves down from the north and turns eastward to run by the city. At this time of the year, in February, the river was a narrow, shallow, stream between the sunbaked, dried up, rice fields. It was thronged with boats. Those bound downstream drifted or were rowed or poled, or sailed very slowly with the winter breeze scarcely lifting their light cotton sails. Those coming upstream were towed by members of their crews on the river bank, who paced swiftly and silently, leaning to the towing line.

The river ran between banks 10ft high. On either side the dried up rice fields stretched for half a mile or more before they were broken up by small islands of higher ground, perhaps 15-20ft above the level of the plain. Each of these islands was thickly wooded, and among the trees were the huts of homesteads (page 33). The low lying rice fields lapped at the shores of these islands like the waters of a placid summer sea. They wound between them like creeks among the woods.

In the empty, desolate basin the almost bare fields were each separated from the next by a low narrow ridge of earth. Through the middle of them the river wound its way, invisible between its banks, marked only by white and coloured sails apparently travelling over the dry ground. The plain looked unreal, like an ocean bed exposed by some calamity of the tides. There was nothing to smooth the transition from the empty rice fields to the wooded islands, teeming with people and animals. These were like small atolls in a flat, grey sea. The vivid greens of the undergrowth and the tall palm trees enhanced this impression.

The strange feeling this open land gave of being something improperly revealed was only natural. For six months of the year it was anything from 3 to 12ft under water. The sweating men on the towlines of the boats were walking across the bed of a lake temporarily exposed. The vegetables growing for the Dacca market in little fields protected by high bamboo fencing, the frames where fishing nets were being made, the motor lorry taking a load of straw from a boat's cargo, the flock of black goats driven by a ragged boy down the river bank, were all there, like ourselves, on sufferance.

Soon the snows of Tibet and South China and the Eastern Himalayas would begin to melt off the lower slopes of the mountains. Four rivers which run through parallel gorges in Sikang, separated by mountains eighteen thousand feet high, would begin to rise.

One of them, the Tsangpo, turns south-west through the Abor hills into a broad valley. Here it is called the Dikang or Dibang. Turning west again it enters the deep slot between the end of the Himalayas and the hills of North Burma. Named here for the first time the Brahmaputra it flows almost due west through north-eastern India and then turns south to enter East Pakistan and flows down (changing its name two or three times on the way) through the plain, across the Tropic of Cancer and out into the Bay of Bengal.

In May the first rise of this last river would bring the water lapping up to the edges of the rice fields, and the plain would be broken by a score of water channels, now dry. This would happen all over the southern and eastern parts of the country, for much of East Pakistan comprises in greater or lesser degree this pattern of wooded islands raised above low ground which floods for many months of the year.

Then the north westers would come in April and May. These are violent storms which occur locally over East Pakistan. Modern meteorological theory ascribes them to the fact that East Pakistan is the meeting place of two great air masses, the Indian continental mass and the South East-Asian maritime mass. In the early summer when the sun is heating up the land and the sea again, instability develops where these two worlds meet, and resolves itself in dramatic and spectacular thunderstorms.

As seen from a house in a prosperous suburb of Dacca such a storm begins when, towards the end of the long hot afternoon when the trees have been still, the birds silent, and even the noise from the distant main road has seemed less, there is an abrupt, sudden, stirring of the curtains, a sigh of wind across the veranda and then a violent rattling of the open windows. The intense bright sunlight of the early summer is cut off by rapidly moving banks of black clouds. The wind becomes stronger until the heaviest trees are beginning to move their upper branches. Then there may be heard a distant rushing sound like the noise of far off breakers. This is the rain front, the true storm front. Travelling fast, perhaps at thirty miles an hour, it presents the aspect of a solid wall of water advancing across the countryside. Just before it arrives a wave of cold air pushes aside the stale dry heat and there is a sudden shock of bracing cool, like entering an air conditioned room. Before the rain envelops everything, the tall solid salwood trees toss and rock and are even torn down, the world is filled with the roar of wind and rain and the crack of nearby thunder, through which come the thin cries of the people caught in the streets. Sometimes I have seen the day turn as black as a moonlit night, brightened by the almost continuous flicker of lightning. Often, of course, the electricity fails at the height of the storm as a tossing tree sweeps away a power cable. Soon the roads are littered with leaves and twigs and branches, and first the gutters and then the roads themselves become torrents.

The storm blows over as quickly as it began. In the bazaars people begin to prop up fallen bamboo walls and salve floating property, the rubbish heaps begin to steam and the sodden cattle come out from under whatever shelter they have found. The boats which have been pulled hastily into the river banks by their weather-wise crews are pushed off again, and baled out as they go. A few, caught in the middle of a big river, may have had a miserable time, drifting for miles in a steep short sea and rain filled semi-darkness. Very rarely, one may have been turned over, or overwhelmed and sunk, and a smear of bobbing cooking pots and pathetic bamboo relics rapidly dispersing on the water will be all that remains. Everybody caught outside is soaked through. But the rain is warm and the air is warm after the storm, everything dries rapidly as the sun breaks through the retreating clouds and the peasant in his field, the boatman on the river, and the town clerk whose cheap shoes have been reduced to pulp, are all happy again.

They are happy because the rivers are rising. The north westers may reach the intensity of tornadoes so that whole villages have been torn up, boats have been literally sucked off the rivers into the air, and forests have been destroyed by winds of over one hundred miles an hour, so that the storms are called in Bengali *Kal Baisakhi*, 'the disasters of May'. But as much as twenty inches of precious rain has been known to fall in a single storm.

As the first small waterways begin to fill, settlements inaccessible for months are linked by launch and rowing boat with the outside world again. The jute crop on which the economy of the country greatly depends gets the depth of water it needs to give it a proper start in life. The young plants of the main rice crop have plenty of water to draw upon. Providing the rainfall of the *Kal Baisakhi* is not more than average the agricultural year has begun well, a matter of the utmost importance in a densely populated country perpetually short of food.

But the melting of the Tibetan snows and the spectacular thunderstorms of the early summer, though they damp the parched earth and fill the navigable ditches and bring cool air to break the heat of April and May, do not fill the dried up lakes and creeks and turn the country into a floating world. The great fact of life in East Pakistan is the south-west monsoon.

The monsoon is not a storm, whatever its name might at first hearing suggest. It is a system of weather, a season. In parts of the world, such as East Pakistan, which lie right in the monsoon belt, that fact imposes on their inhabitants a distinctive way of life. The whole pattern of existence is shaped by the circumstance that for three or four months very heavy warm rain will fall, usually almost every day. This fact is the strongest influence in determining the character of vegetation and of the animal life of the country, its communications and, until very recent years, the way in which its natural resources could be utilised. So in the end it helps determine also the character, the art, and the philosophy, as well as the material civilisation, of its inhabitants.

The south-west monsoon of the Indian Ocean influences in greater or lesser degree the way in which about a third of the people in this world live. The exact causes of the Asian monsoon cannot be conveniently summarised. Very generally indeed, what happens is that when, each January, the earth begins to tilt towards the sun so that its northern half enjoys most of the radiation, the great land mass of Asia, all in the northern half of the world (its southernmost tip, Singapore, is just off the equator) and extending over nearly one third of the land surface of the globe, begins to heat up. The great central inland mass which stretches from the Bosphorus to Peking heats up around the edges, the lower parts. The waters of the Indian Ocean and the air over them remain generally cooler than the land, and warm damp air from the south flows in over the continent. It comes as a south-west wind, charged with moisture after a journey across four thousand miles of water.

All around the Indian coasts and the coasts of Burma and Ceylon the first signs of the monsoon, coming almost every day in the form of large clouds, appear late in May. The humidity rises. The days become sticky and oppressive. Books begin to go mouldy. Cameras will rapidly spoil if they are not put away in airtight trunks. Clothes begin to smell fusty if they are not regularly aired. Any movement leaves a film of sweat on the skin. The glass of iced water drawn from a bottle in the refrigerator is streaming with moisture which has condensed on the outside surface before it has been carried as far as the study.

There seem to be even more insects about than usual. People resign themselves to the discomforts of the monsoon and adjust their way of life to the conditions. But tempers become shorter. The manager swears at the clerk, the clerk at the labourer, in the narrow streets of Dacca the policeman shouts at the rickshaw driver, the rickshaw driver yells abuse at the bullock cart.

Over it all there is a tenseness of expectation, of waiting. The rice dealer in the market, the shipowner in his office, the Civil Servant in the Administration Building, the schoolmaster, the boatman, especially the peasant in the fields, even the earth itself, are all waiting. As the days go past the atmosphere becomes heavier and the heat and humidity grow until, if rain is delayed, they become almost unbearable. All work slows down, the very rivers seem to stand still in an oppressive miasma of heat and stickiness.

A breeze blows first from the east and then rapidly shifts to the south-west, becoming stronger. Torrents of rain begin to fall. They may go on falling for nearly two months, with breaks of fine weather. The system settles down at periods of almost clockwork regularity. For days on end it may rain for several hours in the late morning and afternoon, and then cease, with perhaps an evening shower. When it stops the streets steam, the trees drip on the lawns of the gardens, sometimes the whole place is under as much as three inches of water. In the streets and offices cotton trousers or a 'lungi', a long male skirt, are worn with loose shirts. The atmosphere becomes daily more like that of the drying room in a laundry. To the person from Europe, America, or from elsewhere in Asia, who is not born and bred to the monsoon, life tends to become dependent on air conditioning or on breezes, natural and artificial. In the cities, in all those buildings which are not air conditioned, electric fans turn slowly in the ceilings of all the buildings. In country districts the old fashioned rope and pulley operated fan, the 'punkha' of Victorian India, sometimes still sways back and forth across the upper parts of the high rooms.

But the tension is gone from the air. Out in the fields the peasant, who covers his glistening skin with only a twist of cotton about the waist, is happy. The boatman on the river sings as he poles against a stiffening current up the rising stream. The earth thirstily drinks up the moisture and then, saturated, lies under it while the water steadily grows deeper. The unreal plains, the naked, almost sinister, beds of lakes, are covered under many feet of water, the creeks are filled and the water laps where the brown earth lapped at the shores of the green islands (page 33). The jute plants rise straight and strong through the water. The big rivers grow until they spill over and join one another through a thousand creeks and backwaters, and the life of East Pakistan becomes the life of a floating world.

The black clouds tearing across the sky, their bulbous bellies full of storms, the grey sodden landscape, the miles upon miles of rain beaten water, broken by bands of rushing yellow and brown where the silt laden rivers hurry down their deep beds, the rain of insects against a lantern, the speed of growth, almost frightening, of everything green, these things are all full of goodness to a people born into a way of life formed by the south-west monsoon. For they mean good crops, good food, good money for the jute, the sugar, the spices and tobacco. They mean less hunger. They mean easy communications, and fish every week. They mean straw for the thatch and cloth for a new shirt and a new sail for the boat. They mean defence in a court case, or a journey by launch to the district town to seek redress, or an oil lamp or an aluminium cooking bowl. They mean that children will live, that a boy can go to the local college to learn something more than the elements of reading and writing and perhaps win a steady job afterwards, or a girl be settled with a good husband. So great stretches of open water blurred by falling rain, broken by tree-shrouded island homesteads, dotted with black boats shaped like slices of melon, with grey heavy clouds filled with more rain above, comprise part of natural beauty for one born in East Pakistan.

The monsoon sweeps up the Bay of Bengal and reaches East Pakistan about the middle of June. A week or so later it is soaking eastern Asia. It reaches far to the north, but in East Pakistan it is seen at its most intense. This might be said to be the quintessence of a monsoon country. The great clouds, sweeping up the Bay of Bengal strike up against the high backbone of the Arakan, the Chin Hills and the Lushais, and are driven northwards into the narrow funnel between the Lushais and the Khasi Hills in Assam. There they are forced upwards. And as they rise they spew forth rain on to the ground beneath—not in dribs and drabs like a wet English February, not in basins or buckets, but in swimming pools full.

London gets about 25in of rain in a wettish year, but almost the whole of the eastern part of East Pakistan and a good deal of the southern parts of the area west of the Brahmaputra get 80-100in. South of Chittagong where the monsoon sweeps in and first hits the Lushais about 140in of rain fall every year, and up in Sylhet district where the funnel between the Khasi and Manipur Hills is getting narrow it goes up to 200in. Just out of Pakistan into India and on a shoulder of the Khasi Hills is Cherrapunji. Here, at the wettest place in the world 560in of rain have spewed down out of the heavens in one year, twenty-two times as much as in London.

The scale and majesty of the rivers can only really be appreciated by travelling on them by boat of one kind or another. One such journey began overnight, and by first light we were on one of the main arteries of the Brahmaputra. There were at least five hundred sail in sight at dawn. The colours at daybreak were of the most delicate consistency. There were greys and greens and blues, all lightly brushed bands of colour, each merging with the bands above and below so that there were indeterminate strips between each. But the predominant impression of the very early morning was of soft pink, when the sun's rays first struck the low banks of mist which had collected over the river during the night.

Scattered all over it, for as far as the eye could see, like flakes of snow on a blue-grey shawl, their sails faintly rosy in this morning light, were hundreds and hundreds of boats. Some of them were river boats from the thousands of towns and villages upstream and on the banks of the smaller channels of the delta on either side of us. Most of these had a single mast, and from the yards across it one or two square sails arched and bellied to the light morning airs (frontispiece). Each had a shelter cabin of sheets of woven bamboo bent over to make a sort of tunnel where the crew, muffled from head to foot in cotton blankets, for the morning was chilly for the tropics, were cooking the first meal of the day in pots on an open fire.

Some of the boats were sea boats from the delta villages and from the sea coast beyond the mouths of the big rivers. These were deeper, stronger, better fitted to face the open sea than the river boats. Some of them were rigged like Arab vessels with tall triangle shaped lateen sails; some had sails like those of Chinese junks; some boats, ketch rigged, looked, from far off, like big cruising yachts of the kind built in Scotland on local fishing boat lines; while others, nearby, were great seagoing dugouts, carved from a single hollowed log 60ft long. They resembled ships in Italian paintings of the early 1400s with a squaresail on the foremast and a high pointed sail on the mizzen.

The rivers of East Pakistan are a great mixing place of the ancient traditions of sailing boat building and rigging, Far Eastern, middle Eastern and European, and the strongest and perhaps the oldest traditions are those the Pakistani boatbuilders have evolved themselves. Nearly all the boats except some of the bigger seagoing ones were very gracefully shaped, like slices of melon or new moons floating on their backs in the water, but with the pointed stern higher out of the water than the pointed bow. Some boats stretched so far over the water at bow and stern that it was difficult to see how they managed to float upright at all (page 34). Many, with their great square sails and the helmsman sitting high up at the steering oar in the stern, looked remarkably like the boats of ancient Egypt.

This great fleet at dawn was an impressive sight. The hundreds of thousands of sailing boats on the great rivers of East Pakistan, and in the estuaries, and trading on the coasts beyond, carry millions of tons of cargo every year, more than all the railways, the few roads of the country, and the aeroplanes put together. Many times as much, even, as the network of river steamer and launch services which stretches all over the southern and eastern parts of East Pakistan. The rivers are the real highways of this part of Pakistan. Everyone is more or less of a boatman.

The way of life of over 40 million people is governed in large part by inland water. Many of them have to take to boats, not merely to move from village to village, but even from house to house when the south-west monsoon roars down on the coast and the rivers rise and rise until the whole country seems awash.

When we sighted the great fleet at dawn I was a passenger in a big tug, the *Brisha*, owned by a firm which sailed an extensive fleet of river steamers, some of them driven by paddle wheels in the stern, and all, even fine new modern ships, still looking something like the classic steamboats of the Mississippi of Mark Twain. These steamers, some of which carry hundreds of passengers and several hundred tons of cargo and yet are able to float in water only a few feet deep, find their way over much of the vast system of waterways, mostly on regular scheduled services. Without them the country's economy would function only with great difficulty. For thousands of square miles in East Pakistan where the rivers are the only highways the steamers are the only regularly timed visitors.

But the steamers do not confine themselves to the inland parts of the waterways. The estuaries of the big rivers are like the open sea, and the head of the Bay of Bengal during the south-west monsoon is as rough and nasty a stretch of coastal water as you will find anywhere. It is worse than most, with its intricate pattern of shallows, its sudden savage squalls filled solid with rain, and the fresh water from the great rivers coming down against wind and tide. Yet deep-sea tugs towing sea-going barges sail all the year round up and down the rivers between the capital city, Dacca, and Chittagong, the great port on the long tongue of East Pakistan which stretches down towards Burma.

It is a strange voyage. The little flotilla threads its way for miles among submerged sandbanks through which invisible rivers run in deep channels. Only the low line of green which is the distant shore shows that this is not the open sea. When the banks come closer the thick jungle grows to the water's edge, and even into the water. There are lonely islands where villages of thatched bamboo huts cluster on the beaches and hundreds of brown children rush down to the river shrieking *'Jahaj! Jahaj!'*: 'Steamer! Steamer!' as the tug goes by. No steamer ever stops at these villages. They are cut off from the outside world by the jungle and by the water. The slow pulse of life in them is shaped by a few outward circumstances, the cycle of rice cultivation, the kinds of fish caught at each season, the coconut harvest, the annual storms and inundations. For at the end of the hot weather in October and November, when land and sea are cooling at their different rates, the instabilities which develop resolve themselves in the awful cyclones which, with their tidal waves, devastate these villages of the estuary islands first, before sweeping with death and destruction over the low country to the North. Here the worst disasters have occurred.

No wonder the people venerate the rivers. They begin in the snows of Tibet, or the jungles of Manipur, or the northern slopes of Nanda Devi. A substantial part of the drainage of one of the great mountain ranges of the world flows down various streams into East Pakistan, mixes and mingles in the hot steaming alluvial plain, and rips its way out through the jungle of the Sundarbans into the Bay of Bengal through the maze of changing waterways.

Through the most easterly part of this labyrinth the *Brisha* wound her way with her two great barges first swinging at the end of a nylon tow-rope astern and then, as the channels narrowed, lashed alongside. Her master was sensitive to the ways of the rivers. A life-long waterman from Noakhali, a district to the east of the Brahmaputra, he knew how the tide and the fresh water stream played and fought together. He knew where the slack water lay, and how to keep in the stream from a draining shallow sloping north long after the south going ebb had set in. He knew where the constantly shifting banks would have moved themselves to at this stage in the dry weather. He addressed the barges by their names, personally. '*Aftab!*' he said to one of them when we stopped for the night in a narrow channel between high jungles that looked strangely yellow in the beam of the tug's searchlight, '*Aftab!* Drop your anchor!' And then to the other, '*Mahtab!* Make fast to *Aftab*!'

In the glare of the searchlight before dawn *Aftab*'s anchor was weighed. While the master chatted on his radio telephone with another tug, miles away in the rivers to the north, the small crew of the barge wound up the anchor and its many fathoms of chain cable with the hand capstan on the foredeck. It was an interesting contrast, the radio and the hand capstan, emphasised by the fact that the crew of the *Aftab* suddenly burst into a song something like a sea chanty—a spontaneous working song, it evidently had its roots very deep in the life on the rivers.

Later we slipped by great plains of fresh green young rice, broken by clumps of trees which marked the homesteads that stood on every piece of raised land, and endlessly changing pattern of greens and browns and blues with fishing boats and cargo boats, passenger boats, villages, jungle and rice land.

Somewhere down below in the *Brisha* somebody was rolling out the paste of spices for a fish curry lunch. He was using a stone roller, shaped like a simple rolling pin, on a stone slab shaped like a tombstone with shallow horizontal grooves cut every half inch in its surface to make it rough to break up the spices into a satisfactory amalgam of various kinds of chilli, tamarind, ginger, garlic, onion, bay leaf, cinnamon and coconut. The whole would be a bright orangey yellow in colour, and though bilious would taste delicious when it was served cooked.

The stone roller rattled and grated on the slab, 'clickety clack', and on almost every one of the sailing boats on the river the same job was being done. A boatman knelt on the loose boards of the deck of the living space under the *chauni*, the cover of woven bamboo, boards polished and worn with many years of many crews sleeping and sitting and working there, and, while the mast and rigging strained to the bellied sails overhead, or with rhythmic creaks the oars and steering and sculling paddle pushed the boat forward, he ground and ground away at the yellow spices (page 52). Each boat had an open wood fire in a little clay hearth on deck where rice bubbled and boiled in an iron pot. Each boat trailed fishing lines. No one would think of buying fish which could be taken free from the river.

Page 33 (*above*) The river ran between banks ten feet high. On either side the dried up rice fields stretched for a half mile or more before they were broken up by small islands of higher ground, perhaps fifteen or twenty feet above the level of the plain. Each of these islands was thickly wooded, and among the trees were the huts of homesteads; (*below*) in the monsoon the creeks are filled and the water laps where in winter the brown earth lapped at the shores of the green islands

Page 34 (*left*) Some boats stretc
so far over the water at bow
stern that it was difficult to see h
they managed to float upright at
(*below*) at busy waterside mark
boats lie in their dozens,
beached, their crews hawking th
cargoes in strident local dialec

Two

THE FLOATING WORLD

During the south-west monsoon and for months after it is finished East Pakistan becomes a world of water. It is this fact which has given peculiar characteristics to the human life that is lived there. It is a world of men who live three-quarters of their lives on the water, a world of men who make voyages taking many months, but who never sail the open sea at all. It is a world of colour, the constantly changing shades of the rivers, the pageantry of the clouds, the glory of the monsoon sunsets seen across the water. It is a noisy, shouting, world of busy waterside markets with boats lying in their dozens, half-beached, their crews hawking their cargoes in strident and persistent local dialect (page 34). And it is a quiet world of still evenings on lonely islands in great rivers, when the only sound is the sighing of a dying breeze among the swamp grasses.

It is a world of backbreaking toil at the oar, or at the long bamboo pole, or leaning for hours at the tow rope. But it is also a world of leisure, of many days with little to do except tend helm and sheet and braces and judge tide and wind and current with skill passed down from father to son.

This world has songs and poetry of its own,

> The river has no bank, no shore,
> Therefore, which bank shall I leave, to which shall I go?
> From whom shall I know?
> The clouds array themselves against me,
> The lightning paints in golden flashes,
> The river speeds along swollen with rain,

In the lightning I see for a moment a golden picture
But never see it again.

Such songs the boatman sings. Nobody knows who composed them or where, or when.

It is also a world of storms. Sometimes the rain comes so solidly that you gasp for breath. Sometimes, like a flock of homing birds all the boats in sight will suddenly, and for no reason very obvious, turn towards the river bank, taking in their sails as they go. Not to do so is to be put in danger of capsize by a storm of whose violence and suddenness there is no particular apparent warning. At other times a livid, threatening sky is ignored by the boatmen and no storm comes.

A cloud gathers in the west
And there is a noise there like a roaring lion.
The rope securing the steering oar of my boat breaks!
And the boat goes reeling,
Oh boatman!
Be on guard as you row in high wind and storms,
Sharks and crocodiles are our neighbours!

The boatman's endurance and his knowledge of the rivers is acquired the hard, long way. For more than half the year this world of the East Pakistan boatman is one of damp heat, of heat and a glare that strikes at the backs of the eyeballs. The heat makes the cabin top too hot to touch, the humidity brings rivulets of sweat down every crack in the skin at every movement. The heat seems to stifle the very grass at the riverside stopping places, to leave the cattle stupid, the dogs panting and half dead. Even the scavenging crows seem lethargic. And in this heat, even when all the rest of living things in East Pakistan lie in the shade and long for a breeze, hot and damp though it is when it comes, the boatman rows, sculls, and poles his craft, or tows them at a fast walking pace from the river bank, striding up and down among the paddy fields, under the trees, skirting the edges of villages, lost among the tall reeds.

He first goes away in the boat with his father when he is a very small boy. In most cases his mother and sisters stay behind in the village and till the family land. From this time on the rivers rule his life. He lives afloat on them for months on end.

When he is thirsty he dips a cup into the water and drinks. If a stranger did that in one of the crowded roadsteads, at Chandpur or Narayanganj or Barisal, he would probably survive cholera and typhoid only to suffer both the main kinds of dysentery. But the boatman either dies in childhood or becomes relatively immune. When he wants to wash, which is very often, he does so in the river, going through a complicated routine immersed waist deep at the water's edge. He swims almost as soon as he can walk, with a kind of quick dog paddle which he can keep up for hours. When he wants to relieve himself he climbs out on to the lower beam of a triangle of wood suspended over the quarter or over the stern of his boat, and uses the river as a lavatory. Afterwards he washes himself, splashing up the river water with his left hand. Whether he is a Muslim or Hindu he uses only his right hand to scoop up the rice when he eats.

Because the rivers and lakes are for ever drying up and forming again, the boatman's world is a constantly changing one. The chief navigational instrument he uses in finding his way around in it is acquired local knowledge. The extent and intimacy of this memory of the layout of a complex of rivers, lakes, marshes, islands and villages depends on the sort of boatman he is. A local man, earning his living with a small passenger and cargo boat, perhaps thirty feet long, sailed and rowed with the help only of a boy, will have as his maximum range a distance of perhaps twenty or thirty miles in each direction from his native village. Within that range he learns when a boy himself, either directly or through conversations at the riverside landing places, to know most of the routes and channels. That is to say, he has a fairly close acquaintance with the rivers spread over about 3,000 square miles of country and an intimate knowledge of almost every yard of all the main routes, so that he can find his way along them at night in the faintest starlight, and even, if necessary, make a somewhat hesitant passage when there is no light at all.

Such a man in fact prefers to sail at night, for several reasons. He may, for instance, base his trade on the passenger and cargo steamer service or motor launch service to the local steamer *ghat*, the patch of river bank where steamers come alongside, at his own village. Passengers, or small packets of valuable cargo, come off to be delivered at other villages within twenty or thirty miles standing on the banks of rivers where there is no steamer service. The boatman takes them there. The passengers prefer to travel at night because they waste less time that way. They do their business in the day time and they sleep under the *chauni* during the night. The boatman prefers to travel at night because it is cooler. After all, he may easily have to scull his boat for twenty-five miles. But whether it is safe to travel at night depends partly on local conditions. There are still river pirates in East Pakistan. If the season has been good and rice is plentiful, men of marginal morals will live without robbery. If crops have been poor they will not, and night travel in small boats in lonely areas may be hazardous. So the boatman often prefers to travel in convoy (page 51), all the more so if he is going to an area he personally does not know very well.

Such a boatman as this will have a village house where his wife and children, and perhaps his brothers and sisters and their wives and husbands, will stay. There may be a tiny strip of land for the womenfolk to cultivate while the men are away. But there will certainly not be enough land to live off, because if there was the boatman would not be a boatman but a cultivator, and he would stay at home. To be a cultivator on your own land is good. Boats, in East Pakistan as in other parts of the world, are for those who have not enough land.

A man of this type may spend three nights a month at home. The rest of the time he will be afloat. Each trip with passengers or small cargo is the subject of separate bargaining. He might ask 10 rupees (about 15s or nearly $2.00) for a ride of 25 miles. His potential passenger will offer 5. They will settle for 7 rupees and some rice for the boatman's food, to be handed over at the passenger's village when they arrive safely.

Once during the night the boatman will stop. While the passenger goes on sleeping he will eat a meal which has been cooked by the boy as they go along. It may comprise rice, fish or an egg, a couple of potatoes and some chillies, all boiled up together in a pan. Normally a boatman eats three times in twenty-four hours; once early in the morning wet rice, once at midday after which he sleeps, and once in the night. When he reaches his destination he will take his fare money and go to the house of the passenger. He will squat on the doorstep of the house and he will ask for his rice. His passenger's servant or wife will hand it over, after some grumbling, and a long conversation will follow. The boatman will say that man cannot live by rice alone, he works hard in the sun and he needs salt and meat to keep alive. He cannot earn enough to buy enough food. The wife will say that her husband is poor man and food is dear. She cannot afford to keep idle boatmen as well as her family. Soon he leaves with rice, salt, and perhaps a handful of chillies.

He may find that rice is cheaper here than in his own village. He invests what money he has with him in a small cargo and sets off for home. A boatman described just such a voyage to me one day. When he had gone a few miles, after nightfall, he learned from other passing boats that there were river pirates ahead. He could either wait until daylight and finish the journey under the hot sun or risk loss of his cargo and even of his clothes. He took off his shirt and *lungi*, the skirt he wore for working, and wrapped an old piece of cloth around his private parts. Under his direction the boy stowed all the rice well down under the deck boards and hid the cooking pots and their own food there too. When they came to the place where he had been told the pirates were probably lying in wait he told the boy to set up a great wailing from the bow of the boat. By and by he heard a summons from across the dark water.

'Hey there, boatman, come over here or we will come over there and cut your throat!'

'But I have been robbed,' he wailed, 'river pirates a mile away stopped me and they took everything I have, they took all my rice, my fish, my cooking pots, even the boy's loincloth, look, he is naked, and he is a big boy to go thus shamefully bare. I am a poor man and I am ruined!'

The pirates muttered angrily among themselves and swore at the interlopers down the stream. Some were for going to settle with their rivals straight away, some for making the boatman go with them. Eventually their leader said,

'This is our river. You should not have been robbed here by anyone but us. We are sorry that evil men have stopped you. Here is a *lungi*, and rice, and a cooking pot. Now be on your way.'

My informant said that he and the boy had never paddled so hard and for so long as they did that night. Not, of course, that he had very much to lose. Like most boatmen of his class he owned his own boat, which was about 20ft long and worth, he thought, about 100 rupees if he had had to sell it. He had on board a pot for his own cooking rice, a small earthenware stove called a *chula*, a frying pan, a plate or two, some bottles and a tin mug. He had one *lungi*, one cotton vest, one shirt, one blanket, and an all-purpose towel (called a *gamchha*). He carried no change of clothes with him, though he probably owned one for feast days in his village. If he got wet in the boat, as he frequently did, he just dried off in the breeze and sunlight as he went along. He had a *hookah* made from a dried coconut shell. He carried his tobacco in an old cigarette tin and fire in an earthenware bowl filled with dried rice husks, smouldering at its heart. Matches, and a few tiny valuables and a little money he kept in a hollow bamboo slung under the *chauni*. He had one hurricane lamp and oil in a bottle and a fishing net. 'Come wind, come weather, that is all I possess,' he said.

Some others are more lucky. One hot morning I walked the length of the Dacca waterfront past the great rambling palace of the Nawabs of Dacca, now mostly used as warehouses, and the buildings which had been the homes of great merchants in the days of the Dutch and of the British East India Company. I doubt if the boats they saw were any different in form or in detail from those that lay at the edge of the water as I walked by, though I suspect that in the days of the East India Company they were far fewer in number. On this hot morning there must have been at least a thousand big cargo boats and large long distance passenger boats lying between the old Moghul fort of Lalbagh in the north and the match factory at the southern end of the old city.

There were river boats from Mymensingh in the north, from the rain country in north Sylhet, from the delta towns and villages. They had brought cement and stone, jute, rice and sand, bricks, dried fish, earthenware pots and coconuts. There were fast passenger boats, long narrow shallow *ghashis*, which had brought vegetables and fish in from villages within twenty or thirty miles of the capital for sale in its thriving markets. There were timber boats, lost in the middle of a raft of heavy logs, which had come down from the Madhupur Jungle, or hundreds of miles from Assam. There were Indian boats, the biggest of all, half as broad as they were long, with very round bows and a woven bamboo *chauni* as big as a large shed (page 51). They had brought cargoes from far up the Ganges and their crews would be away from their villages for many months, even perhaps a year. There were ranks of motor launches lying at the river bank, and some coming and going all the time, crowded with passengers from towns and villages on the main channels who had business in Dacca. There were a few 'flats', the great covered steel barges, like floating warehouses, owned by the steamer companies, which take six hundred tons of jute at a time on the long hauls from Dacca to the port of Chalna or to Chittagong in the calm winter weather. There were seagoing sailing boats from the delta and from the Chittagong coast. These seagoing boats had brought imported goods up from the deep sea ships at Chittagong. One had a cargo of sewing machines, bicycles and a piano.

The pattern of boat owning is a very diverse one. At one end of the waterman's social scale there are relatively large concentrations of capital in individual hands. It was always difficult to find facts in this industry. Boats are not registered, there were no statistics of cargo carried. But I was told of men who own over five hundred big cargo boats outright, which could mean something like one hundred thousand pounds as the private capital of one individual. Some of these men, I was told, would boast of never using bank finance, with its controls and consequences. Such a man would not look like a big business man, eastern or western. He would look like a prosperous Bengali Muslim peasant, and live like one.

At the other end of the social scale is the small boat owner with one or two ancient boats, cheaply built, badly maintained and falling to pieces, who earns just enough to keep him and his crews. And in between there are boats owned by big contractors by the dozen; by small contractors; boats owned as one of the enterprises of a joint family; by their masters, or by their masters in partnership with a merchant ashore who provides for frequent charters; and boats owned by landowners, jute companies, or millers.

The owner of big cargo boats either pays his crews a monthly wage, which does not work very well, since it provides no incentive to quick passage making. Or, more often, he sails the boat on a shares system. In the days of sailing ships, vessels in Europe and North America used often to be managed on a shares system. The custom at Appledore, in North Devon, for example, was that the owners kept one third of the ship's earnings, out of which they paid all insurances and for the upkeep of the ship. The other two thirds of the freight went to the master and out of it he fed the crew, paid their wages, and all port expenses. Any balance was his own, and was considered as his wages. Many of the big East Pakistan cargo boats are run on much the same system, but here the owner takes two-thirds of the freight and is responsible for all expenses and the remaining one-third belongs to the crew outright. This one third is divided according to the ranks of the crew. The master, the *majhi*, takes twice the share of the ordinary boatman, the oarsman, the man who tows and paddles and poles, who is called a *malla*. The boys get less than the *mallas*. The biggest cargo boats may have ten men, but a more usual crew is five or six. Small cargo boats and the fast *ghashis* for passengers and perishable cargo may have a crew of only three or four. Of course the *majhi* often has two sources of income. He may be part owner as well as master and take his share from the owner's two-thirds of the freight as well as from the one-third for the crew.

The *majhis* (page 52) are almost a hereditary caste, a jealously guarded guild of master boatmen. A *majhi* is a *majhi*'s son. Though things are changing it is unusual for a *malla* to break through to be master. He is an oarsman's son, his son also will be an oarsman. The *majhi* may be a brother of the chief owner, or a member of a joint family which owns boats. He will have learned his boatmanship from his father at an early age. Later he will have gone to school, for many *majhis* are literate. He may well have matriculated, sometimes he may even have taken the first part of his BA at a local college. Compared with the ordinary peasant he is a master man.

And he has to be. A master boatman in a big cargo boat will often do no manual work except handle the steering oar. He will not touch the other oars, or the tow ropes or the sheets or halyards of the sails, though he may give a pull on the braces occasionally to help himself with the steering. But his is the responsibility of command. He guides the boat through several hundred miles of labyrinth of waterways. A long range boatman does this mostly by a kind of generalised local knowledge gained from his father before him on a succession of voyages in his youth, partly by enquiry as he goes along when he is in unfamiliar channels, and partly by seeking the company of other boats, bound for the same districts. Between them, the *majhis* can find their way. Wherever you travel on the big rivers you will find the boats in little groups bound for more or less the same general destination, drawn together by the desire to share knowledge of the way, for material assistance, for gossip, as well as for protection against river pirates. Some *majhis* may even use simple forms of stellar navigation.

The *majhi* must also do all the boat's business. He is responsible for the safety of cargo. When his boat is discharging he usually busies himself in search of the next cargo. Some boat owners are speculative merchants and will direct the *majhi*, or a broker with whom they work, to purchase a cargo of some commodity which they know, or guess, can be sold for more money elsewhere. But the more usual custom is for the *majhis* to go to the local *dalal*. There are *dalals*, cargo brokers, in every centre of boat trade. They are rich, influential men in the big centres, small time men in the little riverside markets. The *dalal* is the intermediary between the boatman and the merchant with cargo on his hands. He does not take a percentage of the freight, but a fee fixed by bargaining. On the whole, freight rates tend to remain stable for quite long periods of time and there is not much argument about them. Most agreements are oral, but the standard of commercial morality is quite high in the business and in the long run it does not pay anybody to break an arrangement once entered into.

At the end of a passage a *majhi* will take the freight money in cash, but he will not keep more than is necessary for his day to day running expenses. He will send the rest to the owners, probably by post office money order. He and the owners will square up when next the boat is at home. Boats are hardly ever insured and only big firms insure their cargoes. But in fact, despite the storms of early summer, and the monsoon, and the constantly changing rivers and the dangers of fire spreading from the open cooking stoves, boats are very, very seldom lost. Though they may be overloaded until the bow *goloi* is far below the water, the bulwarks raised with a temporary wall of wet clay on bamboo poles, still they hardly ever sink. A boatman very soon becomes an excellent judge of what is safe. Only when he is pressed to go against his own ideas do things go seriously wrong.

The humble *malla* leads a very different life from that of the *majhi*. Basically, he is an oarsman. Depending on the boat in which he works he will row standing up (page 52), sitting on a bench athwartships, or sitting on the gunwhale. Once or twice I have seen men rowing a peculiar, quick, and very painful looking stroke, rising to the feet on the forward movement of the body and falling back into a sitting position on the gunwhale at the pull. Almost always the *malla* works on the foredeck, in front of the cargo and the bamboo *chauni*, in the open, with no protection against the monsoon rain or the heat of the sun. In a few boats he rows amidships, the oars projecting through the sides of the bamboo cabin, which is even worse, because there is no breeze to cool him. In the great boats from the Upper Ganges, with their huge shed-like covers, he may row from the roof. Usually he handles the oar alone, but in the largest boats two men, sitting or standing side by side, pull at the same oar.

In all the small and middle sized boats a boatman may work a stern oar. This is the steering oar over the port quarter, rather like the steering oar of a Viking longship, but on the other side of the boat. It is also used to drive the boat forward with a peculiar twisting, sculling action of which the boatmen of East Pakistan are great masters (page 69). Or the boat may be poled along with long bamboos, the *mallas* walking on poling shelves built over the water on each side of the boat. A small boat may be paddled along. One man on one quarter of a 30ft boat will keep her moving rapidly on a straight course with an extraordinary combined propelling and steering action of his blade. Nowhere else in the world, except perhaps in China, is there such a variety of ways of making a boat move along to be seen every day on the rivers. Often rowing boatmen sing. But they do not sing when they are towing the boat. That work is much too hard.

For long periods, often for days, perhaps for weeks on end, boats must be towed. To clear the masts of smaller boats and other obstacles at the water's edge the towlines of light strong cord are attached to the mast head and not to the hull of the boat. Two, three or even four men go ashore with the towlines. Each man holds a short thick bamboo across his chest with his left hand. Often the bamboo is decorated with a design picked out with a hot iron. To its end the main towline is attached. Usually, though not always, a second line is secured to the main towline a few feet behind the *malla*'s head, and he holds in his right hand a bamboo stirrup inserted into a loop at the end of this second line. This stirrup is usually carried at shoulder height, which looks rather tiring and painful. Each man leans to the tow in silence and strides forward at a good pace. They walk in single file, separated two or three yards from one another. They move very quickly. The boats, after all, are very well shaped for their job and, aided by the steering and sculling oar which the *majhi* works in the stern, one man can tow a 50ft light passenger boat as fast as he can walk. Every river had its towing path, winding up and down the bank, high up under the edge of the jungle, down to the margin of the water among the fields of rice. When they come to a joining place of two rivers, or to a big settlement that stretches right down to the water's edge, each man carefully rolls up his line, the boat comes in to the bank to pick up the crew, and is rowed to the next section of the towing path.

There is no tradition of windward sailing among the river boatmen of East Pakistan. The sea boatmen are different. Among the people of Noakhali and Chittagong, at the mouths of the rivers the art of turning a boat to windward, even a boat rigged with a single squaresail, is highly developed. But the men of the big rivers whose sailing never takes them down to the sea do not think of sailing to windward.

To be efficient their boats must be able to go where the proverbial seagull walks. Some of the boats seem to be able to carry cargoes in almost no water. In Sylhet, among the tea gardens, I saw men walking less than knee deep, pushing their great heavily laden cargo boat along through the shallow water. I have even seen them, on the Doloi river, dredging out a channel in front of their boat with a great two man shovel, made of wood.

Such boats would have to have some sort of false keel to be able to sail against the wind. It is easy to see why the sailing dinghy's centreboard has not developed, even though it was used by the Chinese, so near to East Pakistan, in boats which must carry big cargoes and which are constantly lying aground on soft mud. But I wondered for a long time why the leeboard, the long false keel dropped over one side of the boat which the Dutch use and the British borrowed from them, has not developed in East

Pakistan. In the end I decided that there were two or three things against it.

For one, as everybody who has sailed in a dinghy knows, a sailing boat turning against the wind heels over, sometimes most spectacularly, and a completely open boat is always in danger of filling up with water. Certainly an open boat filled high with valuable cargo cannot be handled like that, and as it is the custom of the boatman to take every bit of cargo they can and remain above the water, a laden Pakistani boat would sink very quickly if heeled as much as she would if she was sailed hard against the wind.

More important, the winds and tides and the flow of the rivers tend to work either together or directly against one another. The rivers flow generally from north to south. For much of the year the wind blows from the south to the north, and for much of the rest of the year from a quarter in the north towards the south. The tides, flowing up the rivers, either press back the rivers' flow and even reverse it (and the country is so low lying that even at Dacca the tides often flow up from south to north in the cold weather when there is little fresh water coming down) or, on the ebb, reinforce it.

So, speaking very generally, the elements tend to work directly with or directly against the boatman. Sometimes the southerly wind will blow him straight up a river against the stream. Sometimes he will have wind and stream with him and tide against. Only on the biggest rivers would he be able to gain much advantage by turning to windward occasionally. But often even then it would help him very little, if at all, for with a swift stream and perhaps the tide against him as well as a northerly breeze at the end of a tack to windward he would end up far downstream of where he started out.

So the boatman rows, and paddles, and poles and tows his boat along. His squaresail or his spritsail is cut soft, with a great sagging belly, like the sails shown in old carvings and drawings of European ships before the fifteenth century (frontispiece), when nobody thought much of sailing against the wind there either;

and he sails with the wind, or perhaps at right angles across it when it is not strong enough to heel over his boat too much.

He is a past master at the art of using currents and eddies and tides. He can work a heavily laden boat from east to west through the delta streams stealing from one ebb tide stream to a flooding stream in the next part of the labyrinth, poling a few miles and then drifting in some new current. To help him when drifting he has developed a special device, the *jal badam*, the 'water sail'. This is a bundle of bamboos with a rope secured to each end which he throws over the stern of his boat and it holds her bows on to drifts more slowly than a laden boat and it holds her bows on to the current, giving her some sort of steerage way drifting slowly downstream while all but one of her crew sleep. Craft coming upstream, and fast steamers, must keep out of the way. In an old heavily laden boat every so often someone bales. He uses a scoop, swinging from four cords, one at each corner, and because the boat's curves are so easy and her midship's shape like a flattened arc of a circle there is no awkward corner to stop the swing of the scoop. So, as the old boat sails along, an almost continuous stream of water is ejected expertly over the side.

Three

LIFE IN THE COUNTRYSIDE

However far he may travel, in the thoughts and feelings of an East Pakistani his village family home is never far away. A friend, Nurul Alam, asked me one day to visit his home country in the delta area west of the main mouth of the Brahmaputra, in the area known as Barkarganj. This meant, first, a journey to Barisal town at the northern edge of the delta.

We travelled in one of the passenger steamers, a side paddler of about 1,000 tons with two passenger decks, one above the other. She was very shallow and could carry much cargo and several hundred passengers in about 7ft of water. The accommodation was divided into four classes. The best was on the upper deck at the bows and comprised a set of double cabins, a dining-room and covered deck space where passengers reclined and read and talked. The second class was in the stern, and the intermediate class was amidships, where there was no breeze. The third class passengers, who were the great majority, lay on their own thin mattresses on the lower deck, anywhere they could find space among the bales of cargo. They bought their food from the steamer's galley and ate it in their own earthenware bowls. They travelled rough, but they travelled very cheaply.

The steamer chunked along, past the fleets of sailing boats, down the rivers to Chandpur, and then across the great Brahmaputra, 17 miles wide at this point and looking like the open sea, and into the narrow channels on the other side. She threaded her way through to Barisal and it was evening before we got there. At one point she passed through a fleet of more than one thousand fishing boats, each with a coloured sail. In each boat two men were working the nets. She passed river banks where the tall jute plants grew out of the water, and mile upon mile of rice fields. In the evening we saw what I took to be a flock of low-flying black birds, about the size of crows. There were thousands of them, flapping purposefully northwards over the steel grey river. Only they were not birds, but bats, each 2ft or more across the wings.

We spent the night in Barisal in an old house with very thick walls and a huge shady veranda which had been built more than a century before as the home of an indigo planter. There was then no road to Barisal and there is still no railway, and no air-field. The town was completely cut off from the outside world, except by water. It draws all its life from the rivers, from the endless procession of sailing cargo boats which stop in there on long voyages, and from the steamers, which are repaired and refitted in the local dockyards, and from the business of the villagers for 50 miles around who travel to the town by boat or launch. A line of old bottle palms with thick trunks stands down by the waterfront, and under them nestle the houses of the few district officials, the magistrate, the sub-judges, the superintendent of police. All the rest of the town is a great 'bazaar' or shopping area.

Next morning we boarded a smaller steamer bound for the town of Hularhat. Now the country changed. Instead of the flat plains of jute and rice, with homesteads on mounds of higher ground covered with trees, the rivers were lined with thick stemmed coconut palms, and delicate betel nut palms so thin and tall and fragile looking that we could scarcely believe that they could survive even the monsoon breeze, much less the savage north westers, to which they bend like swamp grass.

In the villages, which we could see more closely as the stream became narrower, women and girls carrying water from the river in narrow necked, bulbous, earthenware pots which they balanced on one hip, holding the neck in the crook of the arm, stopped, statuesque, graceful figures, characteristically bent, to watch the steamer go by. Children played in the school yards, and, like

Page 51 (*above*) The boatman often prefers to travel in convoy; (*below*) the crew's living quarters under the *chauni* of a big Indian boat from the Ganges

Page 52 (*above*) The *majhi*, the master, and his crew relax while, forward, the cook grind away at the spices for the curry that is the first meal of the day; (*below*) the crew of a bi[g] *pallar* stand at their sweeps when wind and current are against them

those at that remote water's edge who saw the *Brisha* pass, shouted 'Jahaj!' Every so often the steamer slowed down, stopped, and then manoeuvred itself with a great flurry of paddles and a rattling of anchor chains and ringing of bells into the bank. Sometimes, alongside a small town with rows of stalls denoting that a weekly market was held there, there was a proper floating quay, usually crowded with waiting passengers and heaps of cargo. Sometimes there was nothing but a low place in the bank into which the steamer shoved her nose while the passengers walked ashore and on board across a narrow plank (page 69).

At one place the river narrowed until it was scarcely wider than the steamer was long. This was the Gaff Khan, a natural channel which had been dredged out to make a short cut, saving many miles of roundabout journey down the main stream of one river and up the next. The Gaff Khan was full of floating water hyacinth plants, so that it looked as if we were ploughing our way through a meadow. Soon we came out into the wide river again and turned north to Hularhat, which is a small riverside market built on the banks of what is now a narrow, shallow ditch, scarcely large enough to take a river sailing boat. Fifty years ago this *khal* was a main channel down which big steamers sailed on their way to Calcutta.

Alongside the narrow ditch ran a tar macadamed road and at the end of the road a battered taxi was waiting, surrounded by an expectant crowd. It was not often that successful sons of the district returned with foreign guests and we were an excuse for an occasion. We rolled along the road, past the masts of boats in the *khal*, and as the sun set we stopped by a clump of tall palms for Nurul to get out and briefly pray by the roadside. His father, Moulvi Yakub Ali Chaudhury, was buried in a cemetery nearby.

Pirojpur, where we were to spend the night in Nurul's family town house, stands very roughly where the Tropic of Cancer and the ninetieth meridian east of Greenwich meet. A quarter of the world away from London, it is a small township of wooden houses. We were driven through the bazaar, with its two-storeyed shops selling rice and vegetables, pots and pans, medicines, cloth and furniture, past the high school and the local college, the hospital and a great pond from which half the town's water is drawn, to the pleasant open village green, the *maidan*. Around the *maidan* were grouped the neat red brick buildings of the local court, the houses of the local junior magistrates and the sub-divisional officer (who was responsible for the well being of the people of a densely populated area of several hundred square miles), the small wooden guest house in which we were to spend the night, and the local police headquarters.

We were taken straight to the town hall where the elders of the city gave a formal tea of sweet soft Bengali sweetmeats, oranges, rice and cakes made from rice flour, and curry patties. After tea a tiny girl dressed in formal adult costume danced with great skill to the music of a village orchestra, whose melodies, echoing in the dark rafters, clearly pleased the unofficial audience which silently gathered in the hot dusk to watch.

Then there was a curry dinner at Nurul's family town house. Afterwards in the garden we washed our hands formally in water poured from an earthenware pitcher and stood in the cool evening air to watch a little wizened pixie of a man in a light brown uniform of his own design, covered in medals, let off the most astonishing display of fireworks, holding squibs in his hands until they exploded, releasing rockets from his clasped fingers, lining the little bridge into the garden with golden fire. We walked back to the guest house replete, while members of the party quietly dropped away one by one with a 'peace be with you' as we passed their houses, and the big bats flittered from palm to palm overhead.

Nurul stayed on the wooden steps of the house. By and by a servant brought a bright lamp and we squatted on the veranda by its glaring light, and while the moths cast great distorted shadows on the painted walls of the house, I sat and listened to Nurul, stimulated by the familiar environment of his childhood, talking of life in his family village, Halta, some miles away to the south, and accessible only by sailing boat, in which he had spent some of the happiest parts of his life.

The homestead comprised seven buildings, six of them of wood, three of two storeys and three of one storey, all together on a piece of raised land, one of the wooded islands above the surrounding rice fields and the monsoon floods. Five of these buildings were the private apartments of the family—that is, of Nurul's father and mother and brothers and unmarried sisters, his uncles and their families, and married cousins and their families, and all their servants and boatmen. The sixth was the *baitha-khana*, the public hall used by the whole family group, the only building to which strangers were admitted, for only most intimate friends and close relations ever enter the private quarters.

The seventh building was a brick-built mosque. All the buildings together and the yard around them occupied about eleven acres. In the yard were palm groves, mango trees and pineapple shrubs, as well as a vegetable garden. There were also several excavated ponds. One was reserved for drinking water, one for fish farming, the rest for bathing, and fish were caught in those too.

For Nurul the day in the village would begin before sunrise with the *Azan*, the call to morning prayer from the minaret of the family mosque. He would rise from the thin cotton mattress which covered the plank bed on which he slept, wash himself in accordance with the ritual dictated by the Koran and the *Sunnah*, the body of Islamic theology, change his *lungi* and his shirt and walk over to the concrete floor of the mosque. His uncles, his cousins, his brothers and father and a trickle of village neighbours, all men and boys, would join him there. Together they would go through the rhythmic movements of prayer, established by the Prophet 1,400 years ago and not changed since, reciting passages from the Koran and the formula of the faithful 'La ilaha illa-l-hah Muhammadur rasul-l-hah', 'There is no God but God and Mohammed is His Prophet'.

After prayers the little congregation would break up. As dawn was breaking the poorer members of the family and the servants would return to their huts and a meal of cold wet rice, spiced with green chilli and onion, and possibly a boiled potato or cold fish or vegetables, left over from the previous supper. Nurul and his father crossed the yard from the mosque to his father's family house, one of the two-storey buildings. They would eat freshly cooked rice with potato and fried eggs, prepared by one of the servants who had helped the family for two generations, and served by Nurul's mother and one of his sisters, or a sister-in-law. The women would not eat until the men were satisfied.

Then the family would settle down to the day's activities. The father, sitting in the *baitha-khana*, would receive visitors, chance callers from the village who had problems, a land dispute perhaps, or marriage negotiations they wanted to talk over. Perhaps a political question would arise, such as who were to be elected to the local 'Union Board', the council of villages which is responsible for some aspects of local administration over the area covered by several villages. Or there might be discussion on some point of Islamic theology, brought to attention by a controversial interpretation by some visiting *Maulana* or *Pir Sahib*. A *Maulana* is a man who has received formal education in the elements of Muslim thought and tradition, a *Pir Sahib* is a man of character who has earned for himself, whether he has had a formal education or not, a special position in the eyes of the villagers. There would be long and earnest discussions of such a matter, which might continue until the midday meal, in which case social tradition demanded that the visitors should be invited to share it.

Nurul could remember how the beards wagged over such discussions. At intervals a servant brought *pan*, folded leaves of a cultivated creeper which have a sharp, clean taste to the tongue. Inside the folds were fragments of the nut of the betel palm, smeared with lime and with one or two spices added to give piquancy to the flavour of the whole. And all the time several hookahs were in circulation among the group, passed from man to man, each drawing tobacco smoke through his bent fingers, so that the mouthpiece was never touched with the lips.

Meanwhile the women prepared the children for school, for on their particular raised island was a government-run free primary school which operated only in the mornings. Then they would gossip round among the living quarters in the family compound, or make quilts, or read Bengali novels, or write letters to their older children away from home at college or school. Once or twice a week servants, sometimes accompanied by older children, would be sent to the village *hat*, the regular bazaar, to buy food not grown in the family compound, and perhaps an occasional imported luxury.

The family's income was derived from a number of sources. They lived chiefly on the products of the land they owned, the fruit groves and vegetable gardens of the island, and on the rent paid in grain or cash, of land owned in other places. Many families own cargo boats as well and derive income from their freights.

Part of the family establishment comprised ten or twelve workers whose job it was between them to till the land on the island and tend the fruit and palm trees and the animals. They also caught the fish, acted as servants, and rowed the family boat to the market in the months of monsoon flood. These men and women were given huts in the compound to live in and food to eat, clothes and all the necessities of life, but little or no money. A faithful worker, long connected with the family, might in the end be rewarded with a strip of land. Their children would be married at the expense of the family, who would assume responsibility for their welfare as long as they cared to remain.

After lunch, made up of vegetables, fish, lentil soup, and curds or milk—four or five courses—or perhaps a chicken, or a whole goat if there was an important guest, there would be a siesta period which lasted until the afternoon prayer in the mosque. In the evening there might be a village football match, or a fair to be visited, or perhaps horse racing, or visits might be paid to relations nearby. Then there was an evening prayer, just after sunset.

The respected elders of the community would sometimes sit after dark in a *Shalishi*, an informal court, to settle a dispute between two of their neighbours who voluntarily accepted their jurisdiction, rather than go to law, which is an expensive business. At night there might be a folk song festival or a marriage dinner, a funeral feast, or some other social occasion. Nurul found the life pleasant, with its regular rhythm set by the times of prayer, so important that engagements were made in terms such as 'I will see you after evening prayer', or 'We will meet before afternoon prayer'.

Two hundred or so such island homesteads, some larger and more prosperous, some a good deal poorer, separated by the low lying land flooded during the monsoon on which rice and some jute were grown, comprised Nurul's village, Halta. Thus the villages of East Pakistan cover an immense area. They are not so much villages in the European sense as an administrative area in which several thousand people live.

In the homesteads the units of the family lead a partly communal life, but they are separated economically. Property and land is held entirely in the name of the head of each individual unit, Nurul's father, his uncles or cousins, not in the name of the whole. But they cling together, from age old tradition and for mutual advantage in times of difficulty.

Apart from those prosperous homesteads live the small cultivators who in most cases own the land on which their small huts stand. They may have only a pocket handkerchief of land, and a boat for the monsoon season, besides a few coconut and betel nut palms. These will not keep them alive through the year, so they must work on the land of their more prosperous neighbours. They may do this by renting land at a fee estimated on its past fertility, or they may work another man's land, using his tools and livestock and in return take a percentage, perhaps sometimes as great as a half of the crop. Nurul's family employed men in both these ways to work land they owned.

Thus the characteristic aspect of a great part of the countryside of East Pakistan, raised wooded islands in the plain, bears upon the social pattern. The islands are the homesteads owned by the big families who occupy them, usually one to each island. The unreal looking land in between belongs also to these families, but they do not work it themselves. It is rented to the workers who live on part of the products of their toil for other men. The official annual income of these landless men is extremely low, so low that it is difficult for the European, and even more difficult for the American, to imagine how they live at all. But the rice they earn for their work, the vegetables and coconuts from their own tiny strip of land on a corner of somebody else's island, and the fish they catch during the monsoon from the rice fields where they work, and during the rest of the year from the nearest river or canal, suffice to keep them going. They eke out with wild vegetables, which grow everywhere. These wild vegetables are a very important, if unsung, part of the economy.

As in France, fishing is the national sport of the countryman. Every homestead, every hut, has its nets. A landowner whose prosperity and position would make it socially difficult for him to work on his own land will not hesitate to make his own fishing nets and go out and use them in the river, or pond. Fish is the staple source of protein. Without it the poorer countrymen could not exist.

But even they have a recreational life. In the evening landless men will flock in large numbers to see a village drama. The *Jattra* theatre is usually a hut of bamboo mats with a stage in the middle and seats and squatting room all round. A passage is left for the entrance and exit of the actors, who are professional all male troupes who wander from village to village in search of audiences. The plays are mostly mythological with a Hindu theme, and also historical, in which case they probably deal with the early days of Islam in India. Or there may be a *Jarigan* session, at which two parties of itinerant professional musicians will sing folksongs and extemporise, something in the manner of calypso and mostly on ancient themes. *Kabigan* is the Hindu version of the same things, while in *Puthi* two experts will read aloud from a book of folktales.

The village, then, is an administrative area comprising many square miles of homesteads and of low lying agricultural land which is empty of permanent habitation. Its people are of two main classes, the landowners, who are perhaps also merchants and boat owners, who are in a big enough way to do no manual labour, and the smaller landholders and landless labourers who work for themselves, or for other people, or both. But, besides these, there are other members of the village community who earn their living by selling what they make, or who have salaried jobs. Woodcutters collect timber and firewood from forest land and sell it. Most forest is State controlled and the woodcutter must be licensed. Boatmen go away for days, weeks, or months in their boats. There are professional fishermen on the big rivers who own their boats and nets, or who work for a more prosperous member of the community who has a boat and equipment. These may be either Muslims or Hindu, but there are other occupations which are traditionally Hindu, such as pot making, carpentering, weaving, laundering and cutting hair. Boatbuilders may be either Muslim or Hindu, members of both communities may work together. Blacksmiths and goldsmiths are mostly Hindu.

All these craftsmen live in their own huts on their own small pieces of land, on which their forefathers lived before them. Often these strips will be between the homesteads of wealthier families on the islands of raised land. Sometimes a blacksmith or a goldsmith will live and have his shop in the homestead land of a rich villager who will gain social prestige by providing him with space. Often a dozen or twenty families of the same kind of craftsmen who will live together on the same piece of inhabitable land. Mostly such people will work in a nearby bazaar, but weavers usually work at home. In the village community there are always a few superior salaried men, the schoolmaster, the postmaster, officers and clerks in the local government land offices. These men and their families provide an element with ideas from beyond the confines of the village, even though they may come from the village originally themselves, and have returned to it after getting an education in the district town or in Dacca.

Not in Halta, but in many other villages, there are groups of water gypsies on the edge of the village community. They are not properly part of the village, but they are useful and tolerated. Nurul and I once came across a party of these people. There were a dozen or more boats moored at the edge of a winter *char*, a stretch of fertile silt which the shrinking river had left bare during the cold weather. This *char* had just been planted with rice and was covered with the delicate green sheen of young plants.

What first attracted us to this group was the presence of women, freely moving along the boatmen, and clearly living on board the boats. I had only once before seen women on board river boats who were not obviously temporary passengers, and that was in the Hatiya river, far down towards the Bay of Bengal, where we passed a line of anchored fishing boats with lines out, in each of which was one man, who handled the boat, and one woman, who attended to the fishing.

The boats by the *char* were neat and tidy and clearly the homes of cheerful people. The women wore *saris* of bright colours, yellow and green and red. On the river bank a group of them were working. An old woman was making a quilt, a naked girl was tending fowls and another cooking food for the evening meal. One girl was combing her hair and peering into a tiny, precious, mirror as she did so. While we talked with the men, the women frequently interrupted, and in the end they had taken over the conversation, which was a most unusual experience in the countryside of East Pakistan. They said they were *Shandars*. They had houses in a village 20 miles away, but they spent nearly all their time in their boats on the water. There were, they claimed, 782 families of them—a kind of separate tribe living alongside the agricultural community, they paid their way by peddling glass bangles, small mirrors, combs and hair ornaments. They made spare parts for the looms of village weavers and they sold writing paper and pencils. They collected the shells of the river mussels and sold them. They seemed a happy people, very poor, but not so poor as the day labourers who were working in nearby fields. They had their own social customs, although Muslims they did not follow all the stricter practices and traditions of the faith. The old woman said she believed the tribe had kept itself apart for thousands of years. They had no idea from where they originally came.

Such people would play no part in the celebrations and ceremonies which enliven village life. These are communal affairs, arranged by the village elders, though they may be the main concern of only one family. A marriage ceremony, for instance, brings problems of who shall be invited and where they shall sit, what they shall eat and how they shall be entertained. A funeral feast of a rich villager sets the same kind of problems, though there is no entertainment. A visit by itinerant musicians or the annual fête of the village school give rise to problems of precedence, catering, and as to exactly what shall be done, which are settled in prolonged discussion in somebody's *baitha-khana.* The arrangements for a visiting religious leader are especially important. They will probably be thrashed out in the Mosque after the main weekly congregation for prayer at midday on Friday.

Marriages are almost all arranged between the parents of the boy and the girl and usually there is also a go-between who is perhaps a common friend, not necessarily a relative. Negotiations can begin from either side, but when they reach the formal stage it must always be the boy's family who make the final, binding, proposal. The boy is usually in his early twenties, the girl between fourteen and seventeen years old. When the formal proposal has been accepted, then the elders of the two families, and perhaps the go-between, will sit down and negotiate a settlement in money and goods. This is a very serious matter, for marriage is a civil contract accompanied by practical arrangements, bringing two families closely together for all social purposes. Most often the boy and girl see one another for the first time at the actual marriage ceremony, or at the earliest, while the family negotiations are going on, for in most cases the father or uncle of the boy will view the girl on his behalf.

Most of the village elders who play a part in the arrangement of communal life are bearded men who have made the *Haj*, the pilgrimage to Mecca which, like belief, prayer, fasting, and the giving of alms, is one of the main tenets of Islam. Nowadays the journey is perhaps made by air, and even the sea voyage, which most pilgrims make, is a relatively comfortable affair. It was not always so. The *Haj* is traditionally associated with great hardship. Nurul's own great grandfather travelled from Bombay to Jedda in an Arab sailing boat. One of his uncles, overcome by the hardships of the journey only a generation ago, died in Mecca.

To get to his village from Dacca, Nurul used to take the steamer to a *ghat*, Tushkhali, about 12 miles away. Nowadays motor launches can get within 3 miles of the village. In the monsoon the villager uses his boat as the only way of getting from homestead to homestead. Nurul's father's homestead had five or six boats attached to it. There is little work to do in the flooded fields. The main rice crop is planted out in May and June as the norwesters blow and as the monsoon starts, and the crop grows as the waters rise. The retreating floods leave behind a sea of golden rice waving in the cool northerly winter breeze.

After rice the most important crop in East Pakistan as a whole is jute, which accounts for half the villagers' cash income and the greater part of the foreign exchange earned in all Pakistan. It is sown earlier than rice and by the time the floods come it is already mature. It is cut by men working up to their waists, or even to their shoulders, in monsoon water, any time between July and the end of October. The tall green plants—they may be 10-12ft tall and 2in thick—are made up into bundles and kept under deep water for a fortnight or three weeks, while the skin around the hard core of the stem ferments and softens, so that it can be stripped off as long continuous strong fibres. Everybody turns to at the stripping of the jute. Even the women of the labourers and the small cultivators come away from their households and their water carrying, and, sitting in the boiling heat, work eight or nine hours a day to produce a quarter of a hundredweight of fibre. Then it is washed, dried in the sun, and twisted into great skeins.

It is in this form that this so called 'golden fibre' is most familiar to the traveller in East Pakistan. The soft brown hair-like material lies in heaps at the water's edge, comprises perhaps half the total cargo moved by river sailing boats in the year (page 70), weighs down the carts of labouring bullocks, fills the trucks in the railway sidings. The great bulk of it travels by water to the 'baling presses', where it is compressed into tight bales weighing 400lb each, small and compact and very suitable for shipping. Then it is loaded into steamers or the great barges. In these it travels to Chalna or to Chittagong to be loaded into ocean going steamers for export all over the world.

The history of jute is very much a part of the modern history of East Pakistan. Although it was cultivated in what is now the Indian State of West Bengal at a much earlier date, jute became really important in East Pakistan in the early 1870s. Jute is first mentioned in the archives of the steamer companies in 1873 and before long it was to become the largest part of their business. Village areas like Narayanganj and Chandpur rapidly developed into jute buying and baling centres. By 1880 jute was the most important local crop, and it has remained so ever since. At the other end of the line, in Dundee in Scotland, a great jute spinning and weaving industry grew up, manufacturing hessian, sacking, canvas, carpet backing, roofing fabrics and even clothing materials. As the fields of jute grew under the deep monsoon water so prospered the villagers, the boatmen, the numerous speculating middlemen; the Scots exporting firms, the steamer companies, great lines of deep sea sailing ships, and the mills in Dundee. The lines of fine houses down the banks of the Tay grew longer and the families richer. Now, the greatest consumer of jute is the United States, and many substitute fibres and packing materials are competing in the world markets. But still jute grows, brings in more money and makes more cargoes for the boats than any other crop. It is still very much the second most important product of the low land between the island homesteads.

Years ago, the villages of East Pakistan, like those of much of the rest of the sub-continent of old India, were almost independent—self supporting, self governing, the one fixed and permanent thing, whatever happened in the world outside. Gradually this independence has broken down. New ideas have come in through the western style education first made available by the British administration, through contacts made by easier travel, and through the effects of two world wars. Manufactured goods, although still surprisingly few in the life of the ordinary villager, have become necessities. Land reforms, and the fragmenting effect of the Muslim system of inheritance, with its endless sub divisions of property so that all shall share, have begun to break down the old social structure of the village. Now new ideas about agricultural methods, new ideas of local government, new ideas about the place of men in society are beginning to have their effects. These have been much accelerated in recent years.

But nevertheless, the pace of life often still remains essentially so slow as to be almost timeless. The tempo is set by the bullock cart, the pedal driven potter's wheel, the river rowing and sailing boat. In the hot watery plain the jute grows, the rice is harvested and, whether man is there or not, the coconuts flourish. These things between them can provide most of the essentials of life.

Four

THE BUILDING OF THE MONSOON

To learn about the boatmen and their lives, and about their boats, we had to have a boat of our own in which to move about on the rivers at the boatmen's own level, instead of high above it on a steamer's bridge. But what sort of boat? She had to have a shelter cabin of some kind to provide rough sleeping space, and also day-time protection for four or five people against the monsoon deluge. She had to have a shelter the length of her to provide shade against the burning sun during the hot weather months. But the shelter had to be collapsible because it would not be needed from November to early April. She had to be big enough to stand up to any sort of weather on the smaller rivers, and any sort of weather could mean a 40mph squall. She must provide a steady platform for filming and photographing the life of the rivers.

All these things meant a beamy, stable boat at least 18ft in length. Boatbuilding to European design is expensive in East Pakistan, and considerations of cost meant that she could not be much bigger. To keep the building cost down, and also for ease of maintenance, we decided to have an outboard rather than an in-board motor, but it had to be a powerful one to drive the boat at reasonable speed and make her safe in high winds. And because it had to run for long periods at a stretch and be very reliable, and because maintenance facilities were very poor, it had to be solid and slow running.

Before I could place an order for the boat I had to make sure of somewhere safe and convenient where she could be kept. Here the Pakistan Army solved the problem with an obliging offer of the use of an army inland water transport depot on the Dacca waterfront. The next problem was to find someone to build this sort of boat. This was more difficult than one would think, living among a nation of watermen in a country so dependent on boats for its whole economy. To find a river sailing boat building yard is like looking for the traditional white hunter's elephant graveyard. There are river sailing boats everywhere in East Pakistan, but the casual visitor never sees one being built. This is because except for the places where motor launches are constructed, there are no regular boatbuilding yards in the modern European or American sense. One has to know the favourite places on the river banks, where the craftsmen contractors like to build, and the seasons at which they prefer building. They have good reasons for everything they do, as I was soon to learn.

But even if I had known a river sailing boat builder at this stage it would not, as I realised later, have been much good. At its best the workmanship of boatbuilders in East Pakistan is as good as that of a good small yard building fishing boats in northern Europe or North America; and the timber used, teak and other hardwoods, is excellent. It is also quite cheap to build a boat of traditional form. But the whole rub lies in those words, 'traditional form'. It would have been very difficult to explain to a contractor craftsman used only to building the local river sailing boats what sort of boat was wanted, and even more difficult for him to persuade his shipwrights and journeyman to abandon their traditional arc of a circle sections and curves, their long easy, sweeping sheer, high in the stern and low in the bow, and the clever change in the planking at the topsides by which they produce a boat drawn out fine to a point at either end.

But in the end these difficulties fortunately did not arise. In the last few years the building of motor launches has become a considerable industry around Dacca. Motor launch services pay. They are beginning to change the pattern of life in rural Bengal. Like the buses on the new paved roads they provide a means by which people from hitherto remote villages can go quickly and cheaply to the towns, with all that implies in the creating of new demands and broader horizons. They are breaking down the eighteenth century feeling about moving from place to place.

But, although all this meant that there were people in Dacca who would know what was meant when asked for an 18ft, transom-sterned boat to be built, the launch building yards were geared to the production of something bigger and building a small boat there would be likely to prove very expensive. Moreover, I was not familiar with the systems of payment and inspection customary with these launch builders and as they work without drawings or specifications and their agreements are oral, I was likely to find myself in deep water pretty quickly if I went to one of them.

The solution to the problem came in the person of Lutfur Rahman, to whom we were introduced by a friend formerly in the police force who heard of the difficulty. Rahman came from Tipperah district in East Pakistan and in his youth he had studied at Calcutta University and taken his BA. Then he joined the police and rose to high rank. But during his police days he met a British boatbuilder who ran a yard on the Hooghli river and Rahman was fascinated, like many people before him, with the atmosphere of a boatyard, with the smell of the timber and the skill with which the shipwrights did their work, and by the problems of design and craftsmanship. He had some money of his own and by and by he left the police and learned all he could of practical boatbuilding. When the partition of the Indian sub-continent came in 1947 he moved his wife and all his possessions in a 16ft outboard motorboat through the 500 mile labyrinth of waterways from Calcutta to Dacca. The journey had to be made twice. The boat was much too full to sleep on board and so Rahman and Sitara Begum slept on the river bank each night. Each time they did this every night for three weeks.

When I met Rahman, he was living in a little white washed brick built house on the outskirts of Dacca. He earned his living in several ways, one of which was by acting as a kind of consulting naval architect and manager for anyone who wanted to build a boat which was a little out of the ordinary. He was about fifty

'age 69 (*above*) The peculiar twisting, sculling action of which the boatmen of East 'akistan are great masters; (*below*) sometimes there was nothing but a low place in the ·ank into which the steamer shoved her nose while the passengers walked ashore and on board across a narrow plank

Page 70 (*left*) The soft brown hair
material lies in heaps at the wat
edge, comprises perhaps half the t
cargo moved by river sailing boats
the year; (*above*) sawyers at work
ting beams

years of age, small, sparely built, but with a splendidly proportioned physique. His black, slightly wavy hair was turning grey. He wore rimless spectacles and spoke precise English. He was, of course, a Muslim, and his name meant 'The Mercy of God'.

He knew just what I wanted. He discussed the merits of round bilged hulls against V bottom hulls for boats of this size and sort. He decided on a round bilged hull as being more easily driven, and because it would be possible to build it easily by the traditional methods used in constructing the round hulled river sailing boats. This I readily accepted. Because she was going to be small and easy to move to the water on a lorry he decided to build the boat in his own grassy, tree shaded, back yard, instead of on the bank of the river, and to this I was glad to agree, because it would be easy for me to visit this place regularly and to watch the boat grow and see how the craftsmen worked. By following the building of this small motor launch by men normally engaged in building river sailing boats I thought I could learn a great deal about how the latter were made.

I did do so, and friendship with Rahman opened a whole new world of boatbuilders and boat people. To give a general picture of the way the river boats are built I shall describe how Lutfur Rahman went to work to build the launch, the *Monsoon*, as we called her after the great fact of life in East Pakistan.

First he took us on an expedition across the Burri Ganga river to a village called Jinjira, opposite Dacca, where there are great timber yards all down the river bank. Here there are long logs of salwood, smooth and straight as the finest pine, yet as hard as teak and almost as strong, though a little heavier. There are baulks of teak from Chittagong, thousands of bamboos, and piles of logs of other woods with exotic names, each with its own qualities and uses. Rahman searched energetically among this mass of timber, looking for two or three likely logs of teak which could be sawn into planks and frames for our boat. He bargained with this dealer and that for the price of timber, sawn and unsawn, and eventually selected what he wanted, explaining that it would be collected by bullock cart men from the Dacca side of the river in a few days.

The timber dealers lived in little bamboo huts among the piles of logs and we asked one of them how the great trunks of sal-wood, 50-60ft long and so heavy that they floated almost completely submerged, were ever brought from Assam or North Bengal to Dacca. The dealer showed us a timber carrying boat which had just arrived from somewhere high up the Brahmaputra. I have written that she was a timber carrying boat. This it true in so far as without the boat the timber could not have moved. But the boat was only the heart of a great, loosely constructed raft. She was a big boat, very round and buoyant, of a type I later learned to associate with the Indian States of Bihar and Uttar Pradesh, up the river Ganges. Long logs of moderate girth and weight had been secured athwartships, jutting over her sides for the greater part of their length. Heavier and longer timbers were suspended from these by loops of rope. These logs, which ran parallel with the boat's keel, were afloat in the water, just afloat, because they were so heavy that they showed only 1in or so of their 2ft girth above the surface. The Indian boat was, in fact, lost in a great square of floating timber several times her own size (page 88).

Stowed in this way a river boat can move many times her own weight of timber in a single load. The whole mass of timber and boat is moved by the great single square sail, or by oars, four or six of them, worked by boatmen standing on the outer logs. Clumsy and unhandy though such an assembly of timber is, it still reaches its destination sooner than would a raft, if a raft could be made of the great *sal* logs at all. Later I was to see these timber laden boats working their way through the maze of waterways which make up the delta area. Their crews are past masters at the art of using river currents and sea tides to move the heavy mass from east to west across the main run of the waterways, with the minimum of backbreaking labour at the oars.

The logs Rahman had selected arrived at his house a few days later and a few days later again sawyers arrived to cut the teak logs into planks by hand. I was fascinated to see that they used saws of the kind which were used in Britain and North America to saw the planks in the days when wooden sailing ships were built there. They are called 'pit-saws', because in the cool northern climate it was possible to obtain the full 3ft stroke of the saw by digging a pit, perhaps 6ft deep, in which one man, or most likely a boy, stood to hold the crosshandle at the bottom of the saw and guide the blade. Meanwhile the 'topsawyer', the master tradesman who had served his time as pit boy, stood on top of the log, which lay on rollers over the pit, and with great sweeps of his two arms up and down, drew the saw to take a 3in bite of the timber on each down stroke. In my childhood I had heard many stories of the prowess of the sawyers who sawed out the frames and planks when the last wooden schooners were built at Appledore in North Devon in the years just before the First World War. They were spoken of as mighty men who lived on beer and steaks (when they could afford steaks—they were paid about 12s 6d a week) and whom it was very inadvisable to cross in argument.

In East Pakistan there are two very good reasons why a pit saw cannot be used in a pit. The first and most important is that if anybody, even the toughest most heat hardened Bengali labourer tried to do work as heavy as sawing in an enclosed pit he would die of heat stroke within an hour or two. The second reason is that for at least six months of the year, if you dig a pit in most places in East Pakistan, it immediately fills with water. So the space for the up and down movement of the saw and the place for the pit boy to stand has to be obtained in some other way. A raised scaffolding is built of bamboo, perhaps 6ft high, and by the most ingenious use of wedges, props and most of all, levers, a sawing gang of three can slowly raise a teak log weighing many hundredweight until it rests high up on cross pieces firmly lashed to the scaffolding. Then the top sawyer climbs on top of the log and stands there while two pit boys, one on each side, take the foot of the blade (page 70). Because in the climate of East Pakistan nobody could possibly do the physical work which devolved on the top sawyers in Britain and North America the technique of sawing is slightly different. The two pit boys do not only guide the blade, they pull hard on each down stroke. But the responsibility for guiding the work, for the straightness of the cut, the thickness of the plank, the cutting of the awkwardly shaped framepiece, still rests with the top sawyer.

The sawyers were hired on a daily wage to cut out the timber for our one boat. No sooner had they begun work in the shade of the grove of mango and jackfruit trees in Rahman's yard than some smiths appeared. They also were casual craftsmen, hired for the job. They built themselves a shelter of bamboo and corrugated iron in a corner of the yard to house a forge which they set up. Here they set to work to make all the iron fastenings and fittings for the boat except the special staples which join the planks together at the seams. They made up the components from rod and bar iron, sharpening spikes, threading bolts and shaping the iron band which was to go round stern and keel.

Last to join the party were the *mistris*. These were the master craftsmen and their journeymen. They came from villages within walking distance of this part of Dacca, small, lithe, dark-skinned men who were recruited on a network of personal acquaintance and family connections. They were mostly Hindus and they were simple men, but strong and skilful. They were called after their occupation, in terminology reminiscent of the guilds of medieval Europe, by such names as 'Pearl the Craftsman' or 'Red Diamond the Boatbuilder'. Others had simple names like Gora, Gobind and Lal Mian. These men built themselves bamboo huts in another part of the fruit tree grove and there they lived while the *Monsoon* was taking shape.

They marked the beginning of her construction with a simple ceremony which involved bells and garlands of flowers. Her conception was the laying of a keel plank along a row of small hardwood logs, lying like railway sleepers side by side at regular intervals. The keel plank was a little thicker than the other planks in the boat were going to be. It was held firm with bamboo pegs and with short lengths of jute cord passed through paired holes drilled through it at intervals of about 1½ft and pegged into the ground at either end. The *mistris* made up their jute cords themselves when they needed them, twisting the fibres of the dried jute plant by hand as they went along. At one end of the keel plank the stem piece was attached, a massive piece of teakwood rough hewn to shape with adzes and only later cut to its final form. At the other end, a transom of heavy teak planks was cut out and joined to the keel plank.

The shell of the boat was then built up, plank by plank. First the garboards, the planks next to the keel, were shaped and fitted, held in place with ropes, wedges and shores. Some of the hardwood planks which were to lie in parts of the boat where they were steeply curved had to be softened so that they could be forced into position. In Europe or America in the days of wooden shipbuilding they would have been softened with steam in a rough steam chest. Here they were charred on the side of the plank which was to be the inside of the curve in a shallow trough of glowing shavings.

At the first fitting a plank might show need of a good deal of reshaping. It was then scored with a sharp nail to mark the necessary alterations, removed, finished, and the edges rabbeted with a fine chisel. Then it was fitted again and a difficult curve might call for levers, clamps, guy lines and wedges and the combined strengths of all the labourers and *mistris* at work on the boat before it was finally in position. When it was in position it was held there by a system of guys, wedges clamps and struts while shallow slots about $\frac{1}{8}$in deep, 2in long and $\frac{1}{4}$in wide were cut across the seam at intervals of about every 2in. A flat staple of galvanised iron pointed at either end, known to the *mistris* as a 'Patam Loha' a 'leaf of iron', was driven at right angles to the plank face into the end of the slot nearest the keel plank. It was then bent over and forced down into the slot, and by this action the other end was driven at a flat angle into the wood at the outer end of the slot. When this process was complete on the inside it was repeated on the outside so that each plank was joined to the rest with a double line of metal staples. You can see how the planks were joined from the drawing (Fig 1), overleaf. A boat made up in this

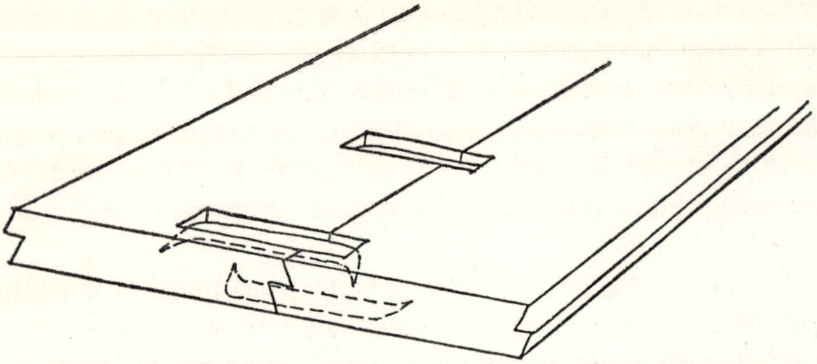

1 Seaming of a round-hulled river boat showing the fitting of the boatnails

way with all the planks joined together was immensely strong.

Rahman directed all this complicated process. He never did any manual work himself and he never touched tools, but somehow or other, speaking the simple Bengali of these simple men, he conveyed to them what was wanted, something quite different from the sort of boat they usually built, the development of her curves and surfaces strange to them and her purpose unknown. Yet they built her, and her shell grew the jackfruit trees. We could see she was going to be a beautiful job.

As soon as a plank had been joined to its neighbour the clamps were removed and the struts and guylines kept it in position while the next plank was fitted, shaped and fastened. The planks were added in pairs, one at each side. This helped to produce a symmetrical hull. A constant check was kept on the hull shape by measuring with a stick from a thin line suspended from the inside of the stem to the inside of the transom. The planking was so developed that by the measure of this stick the distance from the centre line to the planking at the same distance from the keel plank on either side was the same. No moulds of any kind were used, not even the single mould of British clinker building. The shell of the boat was shaped by eye and jute stick. It was a process akin to sculpture, as Ole Crumlin-Pedersen has said of the similar work of old Scandinavian builders.

When she was fully planked up the *Monsoon* was a strong

wooden shell supported by struts and held down by guylines. She looked lovely, to the eyes of the owners, even then. She had a sloping stem from which the powerful bows filled away in just the right curve. Her sheer was sweet and her midships section had just the right fullness to provide stability and seaworthiness.

Now the time had come to insert the frames, the ribs which would strengthen the boat and hold the shell of planks in shape. Rahman explained that he was going to frame her in the locally traditional fashion. The frames were going to be in three separate pieces, not a continuous U shape, like the frames of European boats, but a floor piece to stretch across the keel and join up the planks at the bottom of the boat, a corner piece at the turn of the bilge where the boat's sides turned upward, and a rib, to strengthen her sides. *Baka*, *kunia* and *gocha* he called them in Bengali boatbuilding terminology. He explained that, far from being joined together into a continuous frame they would not even touch one another.

The general shape of the frame pieces one by one was obtained by bending a bar of soft iron around inside the shell of the *Monsoon.* The outline of the part of the frame that was wanted was then sawn out with a handsaw—if our boat had been a big cargo boat a pit saw would have been used. The grown frames of high grade American or European boatbuilders are hardly ever used in East Pakistan, even in the best boats, because the local boatbuilding timbers run straight, sometimes for lengths of 60-70ft. So the separate pieces that make up the frames were cut out of very heavy planking. The rough frame was then fitted and shaped with adze and axe to the proper finished shape of subtle, twisting curves. This was one of the most difficult parts of the old wooden shipwrighting, shaping the frames to the proper 'bevel' as it was called. The method of boatbuilding used in East Pakistan, shaping the planking first and making the frames to fit afterwards, made this part of the operation a good deal easier.

For the reader who knows how boats are built in Europe and America will have noticed that the Bengali system is the exact reverse of that with which he is familiar. In the western hemisphere smooth planked boats and ships are almost invariably built by shaping the ribs and erecting them, standing upright along the keel like the skeleton of a gigantic animal, and then bending the planks around them to make the skin of the boat. In watching the *Monsoon* grow we had been admitted to the inner mystery of something much older, a way of thinking about boats which, though we were to learn that the construction of the big cargo carrying river boats was in fact very sophisticated, was more fundamental, stretching further back into the roots of humanity's conquest of water. Rahman's friends, Gora, Gobind and Lal Mian, thought of a boat not as a strong framework with a waterproof skin of planks stretched across it but as a hollow vessel, a spoon shape of thin timber, reinforced, if need be, with cross pieces and ribs. But to them these were incidental accessories. They did not even care very much how the vessel of timber was made up. They thought of it as a whole, a complete shape of delicate curves. They worried about the curves, but not about what we would have called good boatbuilding practice. Because we thought of a boat as a skin of planks miraculously more or less keeping the water out we wanted these planks to be long and straight and to correspond, one for one, on either side. Rahman knew we thought like that and he persuaded Gora, Gobind and Lal Mian to humour us. But they would just as happily have built from odds and ends of timber with the liberal use of short planks to fill the gaps. Indeed, in building an ordinary river sailing boat they would have had to have done that to some extent because her peculiar shape does not allow of the use only of long runs of planking.

Once the frames were in the *Monsoon* was soon finished. With deck beams, a short deck forward and waterways round the sides, a shelter cabin with an adjustable windscreen taken from a wrecked jeep, floorboards, and a coat of grey paint lined with red and green, she was ready for the water. She travelled on a lorry to the river bank and with little ceremony she was pushed in and dragged through muddy shallows to the main stream. She floated right on her painted waterline. Unless you have had a boat built under your eyes, watched her grow and seen the problems and pains of her gestation, seen her come into being and float, you can never quite imagine the sort of pleasure it all gives when she first lies in her own element. The outboard motor arrived shortly before the boat was launched and it worked for months on end with little or no attention. We also had oars; a six-pronged grapnel, weighing about 40lb, for an anchor, together with fenders, and life jackets. We were in all respects ready for the rivers.

The smiths went back to their village. The sawyers had long since gone on to their next job. The little bamboo huts under the fruit trees fell into decay soon after the rains began. Within a month or two you could never tell that a boat had ever been built in the yard behind Rahman's house. Gora, Lal Mian and Gobind went about their proper business of building river cargo sailing boats. They went to a contractor near the Mirpur Bridge outside Dacca who had undertaken to construct a series of big cargo boats of the type locally known as a *pallar* for a local landowner with a business in transporting sand from the Mirpur area to Dacca. These boats were about forty feet long and eighteen or twenty feet broad. Shallow and massively constructed they could carry a big cargo.

The boats were built on a mudbank at the edge of the river, so that when the mountain snow melted and the north-westers came with their rains and the rivers began to rise a little they would only have to be pushed a few feet into the water. Perhaps the last boat would not have to be launched at all. She would float off and be carried away by the river rising around her. Many boats are built in the cool dry weather on land which will be covered when the rains come, so that they need not be moved to the water.

They were started with a keel plank, just as the *Monsoon* had been, but this plank was forced up at either end with baulks of timber into a steep curve, and into it were dovetailed massive shaped timber blocks, and boat's *golois*. Much care was taken over the curve of the keel plank, because on this the final shape of the finished boat largely depended. Then the planks were added one by one at each side as they had been with our little boat (page 87), softened with fire where necessary, and bent, where steep bending was necessary, as it was in some parts of the bow and stern, with a kind of portable horizontal windlass which was put up alongside the growing boat.

When the planking was almost, but not quite, complete the horizontal deck beams were fitted, many of them, close together, at bow and stern, fewer and more widely spaced amidships, where the sand cargo was to be heaped up. The deck beams projected through the sides of the hull and they were left long at bow and stern so that the shaped ends could be used for mooring ropes and securing points for the lashings of the steering oar. After they had been fitted the planking was completed and the frames shaped and fitted, *baka*, *gocha* and *kunia*, all quite separate from one another, in regular pattern down the length of the boat. Then the boat was given a coating of protective tarry oil prepared from timber resin. She was covered with the same preparation all over, inside and out, above and below the waterline.

She might easily have been decorated with bands of vivid colour, orange, red, blue, as many Pakistani boats are. She might have had bands of copper nailed to her *golois* to shine bright in the river light, or lines of heavy headed copper or brass studs. She might easily have had eyes painted on each side of her bows (Figs 2 & 3), for the great majority of the boats of East Pakistan are decorated with these eyes, either lined out in paint or cut out of

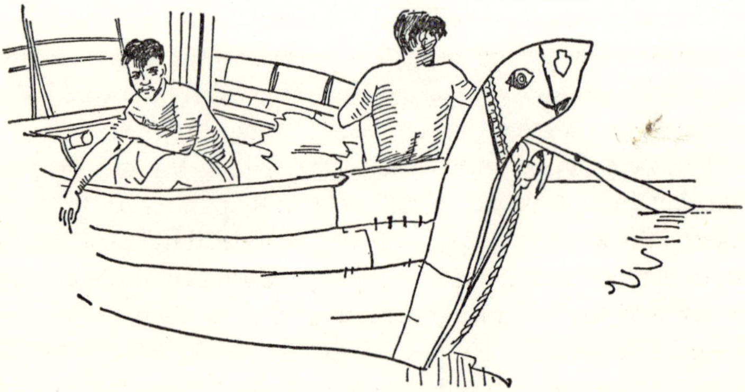

2 Painted eyes on a boat from Tippera

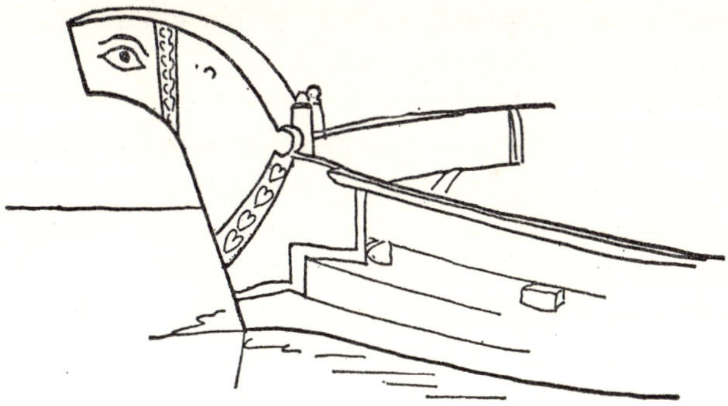

3 Shaped and painted *goloi* of a boat from Tippera

thin copper, or indicated with brass studs. Many boats have them on the stern as well.

The painting of eyes on boats is still very common. I have noticed what look like vestiges of eyes in the decorations of fishing boats in northern Scotland, in north Devon, on the three coasts of France. I have seen them more complete on Italian fishing boats, on Greek spongers and Turkish trading craft, in the Red Sea and the Persian Gulf. In a rudimentary form they appear on the bows of the river boats of north-West Pakistan. I have seen them on boats in Singapore, Bangkok, Hong Kong and, in a vestigial form again, for the idea that a boat is so possessed of her own spirit that she must see seems to have died out earlier in temperate northern climates, in Japan.

In fact the boats Gora, Gobind and Lal Mian built on the *char* of dry weather land exposed in the middle of the low river at Mirpur were intended for a hard workaday life and they were not painted much. But they did have a line of copper studs just where the *goloi* joined the main part of the hull and, powerful, well shaped boats as they were, they looked very well when they lay afloat. Their appearance was helped by the neatly woven bamboo *chauni*, the crew's cabin, which was right in the stern, and the long gentle rise of the sheer forward. They each had a mast standing between two posts and pivoted so that it could fold down when the boat was not sailing, and they had great bellying single squaresails, which looked splendid above the black hull on the grey-brown river between high green banks.

When the time to launch each of these boats came, after weeks of work, there was a very special little ceremony. Because the *mistris* at work all happened to be Hindus this ceremony took an essentially Hindu form. If they had been Muslims they would still have had a ceremony, but it would have been different and perhaps rather more formal. As it was there was a singing of songs and beating of gongs. Garlands of flowers were hung round the *goloi* in the bows, red and blue paint were splashed on the foreparts of the boat just before she was heaved into the water. Afterwards there was a feast of rice and fish and Bengali cakes.

As we travelled on the rivers we saw and studied the boats in all their many varieties. They could all be divided into two great classes, the river boats, and the sea boats which went out into the open Bay of Bengal, and each of these classes could be divided again into several smaller groups. Most of the river boats were built in the same way as the *Monsoon*, but some of them had no frames at all and the planking of these boats was much thicker than that of the boats with frames. Some river boats were clinker or lapstrake built and we found a whole series of these of increasing size and complexity of construction, starting at the lower end of the scale of development with a dugout canoe with planks added to the sides to make it deeper and able to carry more and ending at the upper with the sort of large cargo boat shown on page 87. This was a particularly interesting discovery because until then most authorities had been inclined to regard the clinker built boat as indigenous to Europe. I shall describe all these boats in detail in the next chapter.

Five

THE BOATS

This chapter is a contribution to what Sir Alan Moore in *The Last Days of Mast and Sail* called 'nautical comparative anatomy'.

All the hundreds of thousands of boats on the rivers and coasts of East Pakistan can be divided into two great groups. The first, numerically by far the largest, comprises the river boats. The second is made up of sea-going boats. The sea-going boats are often to be seen on the rivers, but the river boats adventure into the open sea only briefly during the cool months of steady gentle northerly winds about the turn of the year. Each of these two main groups can be further divided by the way the boats are built.

RIVER BOATS

Every river boat we saw in East Pakistan could be classified, by the system on which she was constructed, as one or other of six types. Further observations in districts we were not able to visit may reveal further types of boat, but they are likely to be small and restricted in their working range. We saw no boats in the big centres where long distance cargo vessels congregate which did not fit exactly into one of the following six classifications:

Class 1: The round-hulled smooth skinned boats (binekata)

The late James Hornell, a nautical archaeologist of great distinction who was Inspector of Fisheries at Madras for many years, described the general appearance of the boats of the first of these six classes in his book *Water Transport* and more fully in two articles, 'The fishing methods of the Ganges' and 'The boats of the Ganges', published in the Memoirs of the Asiatic Society of

Bengal at Calcutta in 1924. His is almost the only description of these boats to have been published so far. He pointed out the general similarity of form of these boats, with low bows and high stern, the overhangs above the water at either end sometimes making up as much as a third or even more of the boat's total length. He drew attention to the general use of the quarter oar, often fitted with a short arm or tiller for steering, and to the use of a form of partly balanced quarter rudder in larger craft. He mentioned the general use of the squaresail and the spritsail, and the occurrence of oculi. He pointed out that the river boats of this part of South Asia today look (superficially) very much as some of the boats of ancient Egypt are believed to have looked, so that the Ganges today, he said 'presents a scene much more like that common on the Nile in the days of the Pharaohs than its present day aspect'. (Hornell, like some earlier writers, used the term 'Ganges' in a general sense to describe the whole Brahmaputra-Ganges-Meghna river system.) Other writers have drawn the same parallel with the appearance of the boats of ancient Egypt. Hornell went on to quote this similarity in the general appearance of boats in support of a theory of the common racial origins of the early inhabitants of the Nile and Ganges Valleys. Later writers have supposed that because some boats of the Indus have something of the same appearance in profile (though as I shall explain in a later chapter they are as completely different in construction and hull form as boats could be) there may be a common origin for the boats of East and West Pakistan as well as for the Tigris, the Euphrates and the Nile. To provide information which may discourage such hypotheses it is therefore time to describe the construction of the *binekata*. (See pages 177-81 for a description of the construction of some of the various boats in common use on the Indus.)

But we ought first to look very briefly at some questions of nomenclature. Hornell gave the names of twenty-three different varieties of Bengal river boats, though many of his names are not recognised or used by boatmen in the districts which have become East Pakistan. It is indeed difficult to find names to give to the many different types, though there are certain names which are in common use. These include *badjra*, *bachari*, *bheddi* (as I shall show later this same word is used to name a type of sea-going fishing boat in West Pakistan), *gayna*, *ghashi*, *ghosti*, *kosh*, *pinish*, *pansi*, but these terms are used for different types of boat. There are also a few names which are used consistently for the same types of boat and I shall use some of these in this chapter. Those which are most widely recognised are *pulwar*, or, more accurately, *pallar*, for the big, beamy, full-ended cargo boat of the type which is most highly developed in Dacca district, and *ghashi*, for a long, narrow, shallow, swift boat for passengers and perishable cargoes. But there are many boats even of these general types

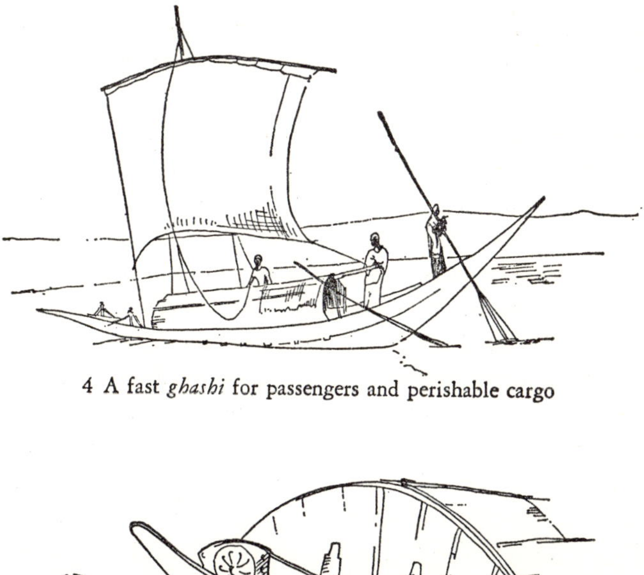

4 A fast *ghashi* for passengers and perishable cargo

5 Bows of a fast boat from Barisal

which do not fall into either category. One boatman whom I asked if his vessel was a *pallar* or a *ghashi* replied that he had never thought about it, but he supposed she must be a little of each. The boatbuilding *mistris* have their own terminology and their classification of boats is probably closer and more complete than that of the boatmen. When I took the photograph on which the drawing in Fig 9 was based I asked the *mistri* what sort of boat he was repairing and he replied that she was 'a big *pallar-ish* crook ended one'.

Structure

All the *binekata*, whatever their hull form and whatever their size—and they vary from 10 to 80ft, or even more, in length and from the extremes of apple bowed roundness to boats which are drawn out literally to a point at either end—appear, as far as we were able to determine in examining several hundreds of them closely and many more less thoroughly, to have four common characteristics:

They are round bottomed and of shallow draft, without keels, though the central plank may be a little thicker than the rest.

The extreme ends of the boat are raised above the water and terminate in shaped solid blocks of wood known widely in East Pakistan as *golois*. In a few of the larger types of boat, including some *pallars*, these *golois* are made up as plank built boxes. In a very few others, such as the great *jhongs* from Mymensingh district the planking is brought up as if to run into *golois* which are in fact not there and the extreme ends of the boat are left open. In the big smooth skinned boats which come down the Ganges to East Pakistan from the Indian States of Bihar and Uttar Pradesh, the *goloi* is vestigial and serves no real structural function. But in the great majority of the smooth skinned river boats the solid *goloi*, pointed, rounded, or shaped like a flattened wedge, is the very logical means by which the boat's shape is completed at either end and an essential part of her structure. The shape of the *golois* and the angle at which they are set often give a reliable guide as to the district of origin of the boat. The *golois* of fast

Page 87 (*above*) Fitting a plank at the bow of a big cargo boat under construction; (*below*) a big clinker built cargo boat discharging cargo

Page 88 (*above*)
Indian boat was, in
lost in a great squa
floating timber se
times her own size;
fitting a side plank
dugout at the begi
of the sea fishing s

ghashis stretch like dragons' necks over the water (Figs 4 & 5). Boats from Sylhet district often have tall, thin, almost vertical *golois* (Figs 6 & 7). Others from the same district, small boats used for ferrying and fishing, have a spade-like *goloi* (Fig. 8). Some boats from Khulna have a tall curved *goloi* of great beauty (Figs 17 & 18).

The planks which form the skin of the boat are joined together edge to edge with iron staples. (See pages 75-6.)

Some boats are frameless, or have only a few floor timbers, but the great majority have frames which are inserted after the planking is almost complete. Depending on the size of the boat these frames are in two or three parts, floor timbers, which in some districts are called *baka*, side frames which are called *gocha*, and first futtocks at the turn of the bilge which are called *kunia*. These parts are *never* joined to one another. They of course overlap, but are usually widely separated in a regular pattern down the length of the boat. Besides these frames the boats have cross beams supporting loose decks, and they have stringers. The number of all these timbers varies with the size and age of the boat.

Building

The building process has been described in general terms in Chapter Four, but there are more technical matters which should be looked into now. The more expensive and well constructed a boat is the more continuous her planking tends to be. When a boat is being built cheaply a lot of odds and ends of timber may be used, some of which has perhaps been taken from old boats recently broken up. When such a vessel is a few years old and has been repaired her sides begin to resemble a patchwork quilt, or the famous brick wall to which Herodotus likened the sides of Egyptian river boats. It can be seen from the photographs and drawings in this book that the hull forms traditional in East Pakistan are all variations on a basic spoon shape, drawn out to a point at either end. Such a hull form presents an interesting planking problem because planks running continuously from bows to stern in hulls of this shape would have to be given a long and difficult taper and to be faired away almost to a point at either end, so that the bow and stern of the boat would be a mass of seams and staples and would have little strength.

The ancient Egyptian builders of similar hull forms were faced with a similar problem. It has been suggested that it was overcome by the liberal use of short runs of planking amidships (which might be described as 'midship stealers') and that in small craft the planks at the ends were in this way reduced to three. On the

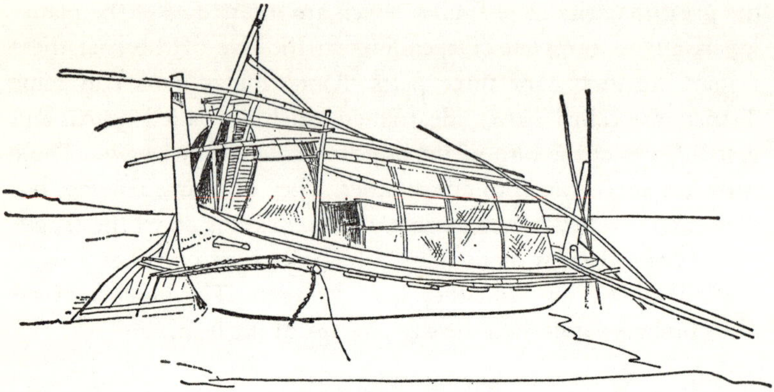

6 Large round-hulled boat from Sylhet district

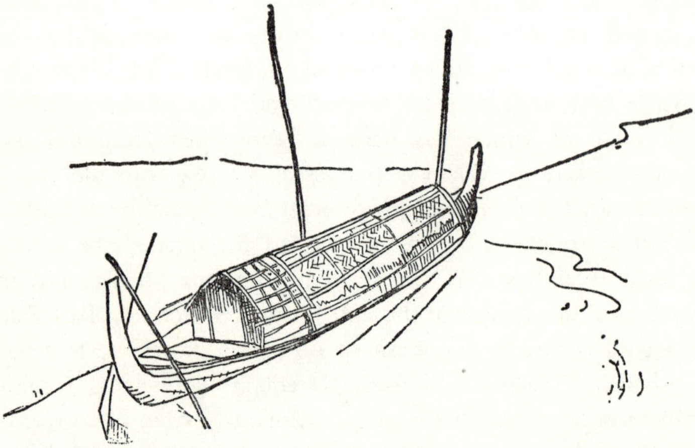

7 Small round-hulled boat used on the shallow rivers of Sylhet district

other hand the Dahchur boats, which have actually survived from ancient Egypt, appear to be a patchwork of odds and ends of timber built up into the form of a boat pointed at either end.

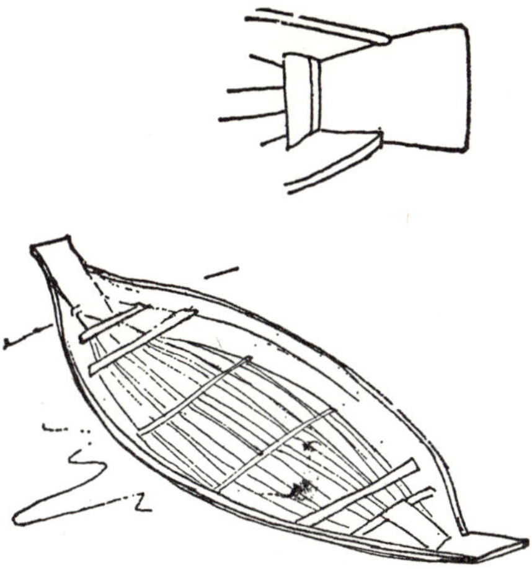

8 Small ferry and fishing boat from Sylhet district

'Midships stealers' are used to some extent in boatbuilding in East Pakistan, and it is of interest that the word used for them, *choragore*, means 'robber plank', but the solution adopted to the problem of planking spoon-shaped boats ending at bow and stern in a sharp raised point is quite different from that of ancient Egypt.

The basic planking is a spoon or leaf shape in which the main planking of the vessel is not brought out to bows and stern at all but is developed so that the ends of the planks would themselves form the bulwarks of the boat if they were carried on far enough. But when this first leaf shape has been completed it is surmounted by a series of horizontal strakes which serve to bind the whole structure together and form the actual topsides of the boat. The system is shown in very clear and simple form at the bows of the clinker built boat from Sylhet which is shown on page 87. Here the stern is planked in a different way to which I shall refer when considering clinker built boats later. In a sharper boat the lower planks come up to the upper whales less steeply and are a good deal fined away at their ends, but the sudden change in the run

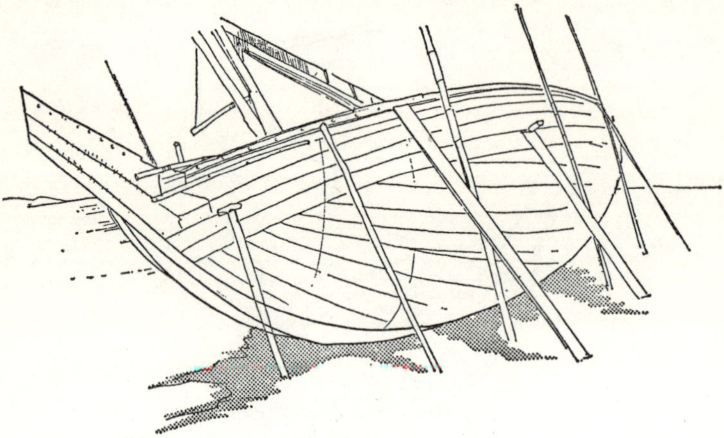

9 A *pallar* hauled out for repairs

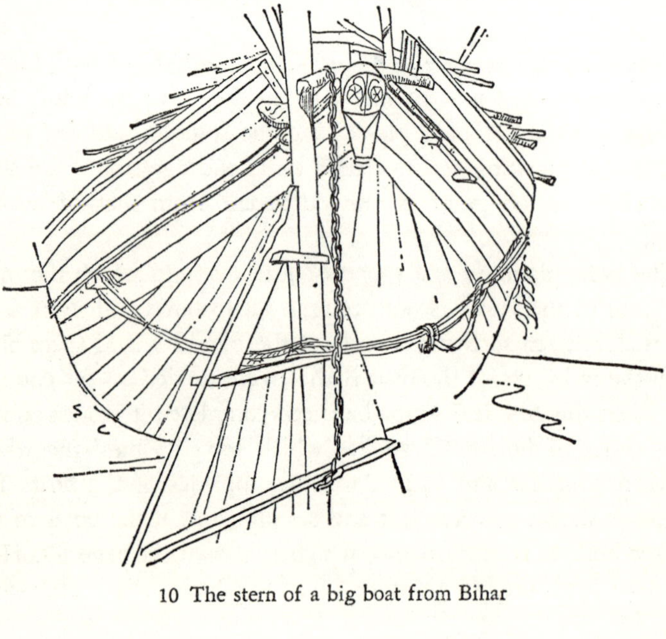

10 The stern of a big boat from Bihar

of the planking once the turn of the bilge is well passed is nevertheless clear and complete (Figs 9 & 10). The number of horizontal strakes above this point varies with the size and type of the vessel from one to five or six, or even eight. Where a boat is very fine at bow and stern these upper whales may themselves have to be tapered.

In the building of the smooth skinned river boats, sometimes after the completion of the planking below the horizontal topside whales, but more usually after the first has been fitted where there is more than one of these, the deck beams are added. Narrow slots are cut into them to give them a V section for the thickness of the planking and V shaped holes are cut into the planks, into which they are dropped. Vertical posts are usually secured between the deck beams and the keel plank. Though these are sometimes substantial they are often no more than turned props, or even battens.

After the deck beams have been fitted the final upper strakes are put on and the boat is ready for framing. In the many boats we examined we found great variations in the number and size of the frames but no variation in the way they were made up from separate *baka*, *gocha* and *kunia.* Three types of smooth skinned river boats appear usually to be launched without any frames, though they all invariably had short sawn floor timbers reaching for a few strakes on either side of the keel plank. These three types are a type of small *dinghy*, a boat from 20 to 25ft in length which is to be found almost everywhere in East Pakistan, and two larger types, one from Mymensingh district and one from Sylhet, named by boatmen working them respectively as *patam* and *daurat nauka* (*nauka* is Bengali for boat and *daurat* may be a rendering of a place name).

Boats which are to be frameless are usually built of thicker planks than those which are to be fitted with frames during building. Even a small *dinghy* if she is not to be framed is built of 1½in or even 2in planking. I once examined a big *daurat nauka*, about 40ft long, the uppermost strake of which was 4in thick. I was told by some boatmen that in some cases boats which are built without frames, or more often with very few frames, are subsequently given framing when, after a few years, they become strained and begin to leak excessively, or when their owners have saved sufficient money to pay for them to be framed. On the other hand the boatmen of the *patams* and *daurat naukas* examined all insisted that their boats would never be framed up. The fact that the planking of these boats was generally heavier than that of framed boats, and that some of them appeared from their general condition to have completed years of service, leads to the conclusion that these three types of boat are built, sometimes at least, with the intention that they will spend the greater part of their lives unframed. We saw *daurat naukas* fitted with very light *gocha* and stringers but we never saw a *patam* with any framing beyond the floor timbers.

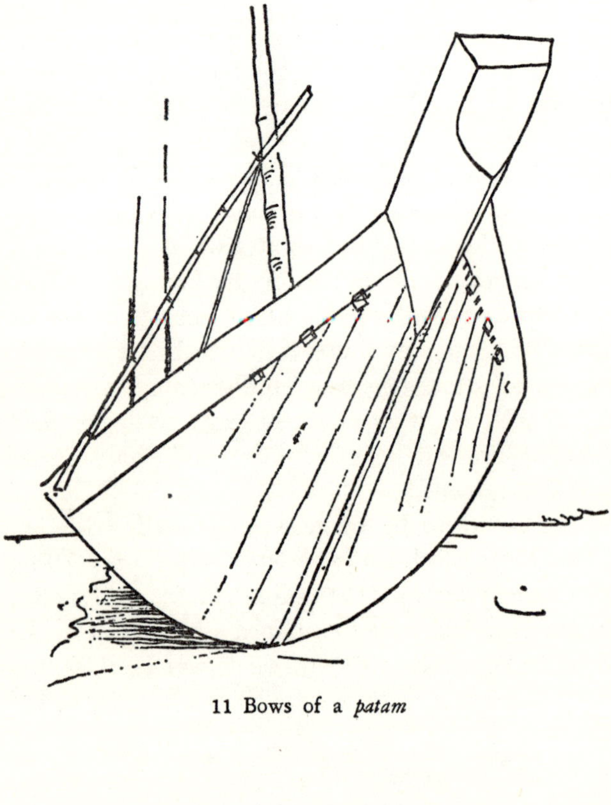

11 Bows of a *patam*

12 A big deep-laden *pallar* under sail

The *dinghy*, the *patam* and the *daurat nauka* are all boats of simple shape. Their sections are a series of similar, semi-circular curves of different radius. Their bulwarks, both in plan and sheer,

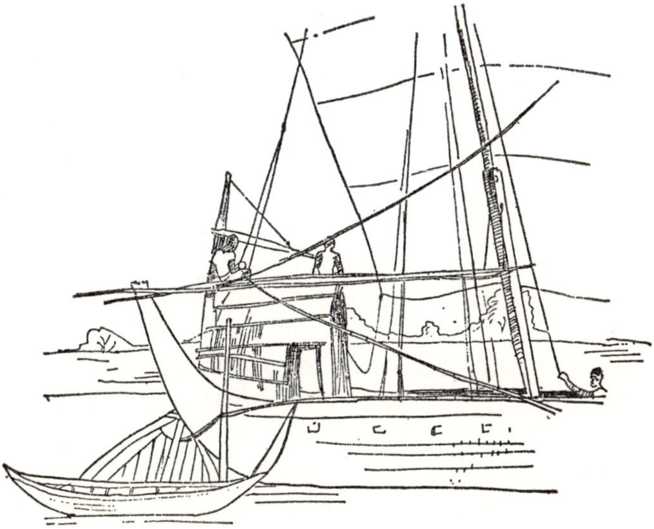

13 Stern of a big boat of *pallar* type from Noakhali district

are long easy arcs of a circle (Fig 11). They have none of the comparatively sudden, sharp, complicated curves of the big *pallar*

14 Rowing a big *pallar*

(Figs 12, 13 & 14) and consequently none of the local points of stress which must occur in the fabric of these boats when laden and sailing. It follows that their shape is less practical. They carry much less cargo for their size than the *pallar*. They are slower and less handy for their work than the larger and more lightly built *ghashi*, and they probably do not wear so well. On the other hand they can be built quickly and cheaply. There is evidence that the *patam* is actually increasing in use and numbers. In 1959 the *patam* was certainly more frequently to be seen on the Dacca waterfront than it was in 1951 and one prosperous owner had a large fleet of *patams* built in the late 1950s.

The planking of these frameless boats is simple. Those examined had only one horizontal whale above the lower planks, which ran easily out to it at bow and stern. From the general nature of their lines they have long overhangs, ending, in the case of the *dinghys*, in long pointed *golois*, while the *daurat nauka* and the *patam* both have *golois* rectangular in plan and shaped in a broad shallow wedge underneath. The largest frameless *dinghy* we saw was not more than 30ft long. The *daurat nauka* and the *patam* may be 50ft in length. The *patam* is the only type of big cargo boat we saw in East Pakistan the bows of which are higher than the stern.

Binekata boats from the Upper Ganges

Although of the same form of construction as the smooth-skinned, framed boats already described, the boats of the Upper Ganges which trade downstream from India into Pakistan have a number of interesting features that are worth describing. There are two distinct types, one from Bihar and the other from Uttar Pradesh.

The Bihar boats are among the largest of all the boats of the big rivers. They are enormously beamy, with very full round hulls and apple cheeked bows (Fig 15). The *golois* have been reduced to mere tongue shaped vestiges stuck on at either end. The boats are planked and framed in the usual fashion, but often with the staples neatly bunched in groups of three down the run of the seams. Apart from their enormous size they are easily distinguished from the indigenous river boats of East Pakistan by the

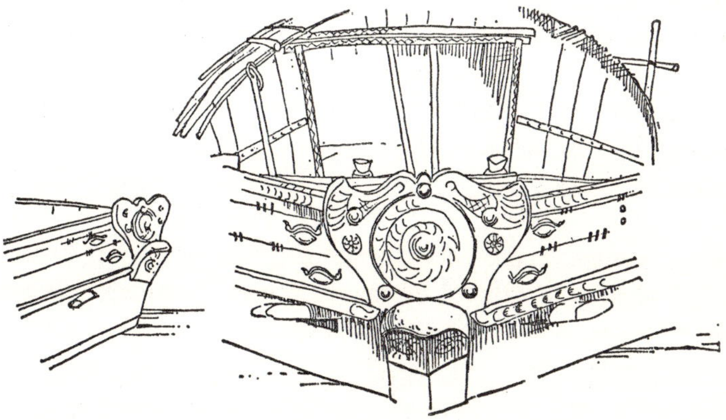

15 Bows of a big boat from Bihar

positioning of their masts, which are in the middle of the long pointed roofed house which occupies much of their length (page 88). Few East Pakistan boats have their masts half-way from bow to stern.

The bows of the Bihar boats are often decorated with brass oculi and with carved designs on the upper whales. Behind a decorated heart-shaped board immediately above the tiny *goloi* at the bow there is often a small shrine for the devotions of the Hindu crew. A big Bihar boat carries over 100 tons of cargo. To work this vast bulk about the waters of eastern India and Pakistan she has a great single squaresail, broader than it is deep, and easily recognisable from its cut. She has also the strength of her crew who work long bamboo sweeps from the top of her *chauni*, down the sides of which high rails are built (page 88). Her mast is often a cut and shaped spar, in contrast with the rough unfinished masts of many of the smaller boats of the lower river, and set in a very tall tabernacle, the posts of which may stretch half as high as the mast itself.

The boats from Uttar Pradesh, though they are still fastened with boat-builder's staples and have their frames in three separate parts, differ somewhat from the rest of the river boats and show outside influences. Their planking is often tapered at stem and stern like that of a European carvel built boat. It terminates at either end in a stem and a sternpost which are joined to the keel plank. There is no *goloi* at the stern. At the bow the *goloi*, if it can be called such, has shrunk to a small piece of wood like a gammon knee, often covered with polished copper sheet and surrounded by decoration in brass and copper strip, studs, circles and oculi. These boats of the Upper Ganges vary a good deal in pattern. We saw some without *golois* at all and with their ends sharply pointed. Some have a straight vertical sternpost, reminiscent of that of a ship's lifeboat. In others examined, the three parts of the frames were in line.

Class 2: The round-hulled clinker built boats (digkata)

In the northern part of the Sylhet district the frontier of East Pakistan with India runs along the foot of the Khasi and Jantia Hills. The rivers of these hills, flowing down through wild deep gorges in the jungle, break out on to the flat plain of the Surma Valley. And there, losing their pace, and with it the life and sparkle and colour they showed in their rush over the boulders and shingle beds of the high valleys, they become deep and wide and sluggish. They meander, merging each with a hundred other streams and in turn splitting into a hundred more, losing themselves in the great marshes and swamps, and emerging only to be lost again in the main streams of the Surma, the Brahmaputra, and the Meghna.

On these rivers, between the lower gorges of the hills and the main streams into which they eventually flow, there exists a complete series of clinker built boats. These boats increase in complexity (and improve in quality) of construction as one travels downstream. They begin with a form of plank-extended dugout in the hills, and develop, through big canoes and small cargo and passenger boats, into a big efficient type of cargo carrying boat which is built in the western parts of Sylhet district. These boats differ from European clinker built boats in many respects, but the most obvious difference is in that the overlaps of the planks, except for the lower edges of the garboard strakes where they meet the keel plank, are reversed. That is, the upper edge of the lower plank is outside the lower edge of the upper plank.

The most primitive of these boats, the craft of the lower gorges, consist of a half section of a pine log, 6in or more in diameter, hollowed out for most of its length, with the ends left intact and shaped into broad, shallow, flat-ended wedges, natural *golois*. The *golois* of the most developed of the large clinker built boats of Sylhet are of the same flat-ended wedge shape.

The hollowed-out log is softened with fire and expanded until its sides are much flattened. The effect of this expansion is inevitably to raise the ends of the log so that the *golois* at each end of the dugout form part of long, shallow overhangs. So much fire is used that sometimes the inside of the pine log is heavily charred and a mass of longitudinal cracks from the expansion. The largest of these are discouraged from spreading by the liberal use of boat-builder's staples. To maintain the expansion, pieces of hardwood 2-3in wide and 8-12in long are inserted across the expanded log at regular intervals throughout its length. The ends of these short struts are sharpened to an edge and inserted into slots in the sides of the log. As soon as the flattened log begins to curl up again they are gripped for ever into place.

I examined a group of these simple boats at Dawki on the Indian side of the frontier. They had been built in the hills by Khasi people who had come down to the mouth of the gorge for the weekly market held on a shingle bank at the edge of the river. On each side of the basic dugout in these little canoes were three

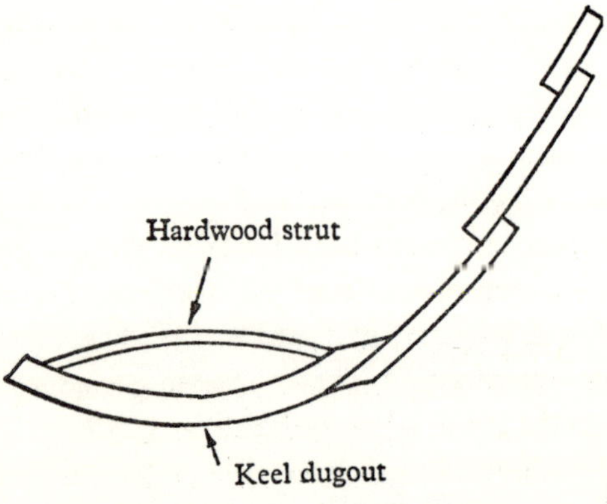

16 Sectional diagram of the planking of a Dawki canoe

planks, two whole and one a fragment (Fig 16). The lowest of these planks, the garboard strake, was shaped so that its upper edge was just level with the top of the solid *golois* left at the dugout's ends. It was joined to the dugout with a clinker seam laid

European style, and the side of the expanded log and the edge of the plank were both so much bevelled as to give as smooth a surface to the outside of the hull as possible. The next planks on each side, which stretched from end to end of the boat, were laid with their lower edges inside the upper edges of the lower planks. The remaining plank, which was little more than a weatherboard to protect the boat where the sheer was low amidships, was laid similarly. These canoes were fastened with ordinary wire nails and occasional boatbuilder's staples. There were, of course, no frames of any kind, but two of the boats had bamboo stretchers loosely inserted athwartships between the upper planks. They were all very roughly and lightly built and leaked considerably. While the basic dugouts appeared all to be of softwood the planking was sometimes of poor quality red pine and sometimes of hardwoods.

Boats of this type of construction, or with a central plank cut by shaping from a single pine tree with the timber of the *golois* left solid at either end, are to be seen all the way down these rivers as far as Sylhet town itself. I have seen the expanded log based form half-way across the valley, though the construction so far downstream becomes more sophisticated. Here the basic log is parallel sided and only a little hollowed out. It is little more than a glorified keel plank which betrays its origin by its continuity with the *golois* at either end and the presence of the hardwood stretchers at regular intervals down its length. Three planks a side are still used, the lower edge of the garboard strake is laid in the ordinary clinker way, the other two in reverse clinker fashion, but in these boats the upper plank instead of being a fragment is the largest in the hull and stretches from end to end. Roughly fitted plank thwarts are used, at gunwhale height, supported by pillars to the dugout keel plank. The largest of these boats appear to be about thirty-five feet long.

Round about Sylhet town itself there are large numbers of big clinker built cargo boats. Most, even of the largest, and most sophisticated, have the keel plank continuous with the *golois*, the whole cut from one tree, and in this they differ markedly from the smooth skinned boats. In the largest clinker built cargo boats attached *golois* are sometimes met.

The simplest type of all-plank built *digkata* boat comprises a thick keel plank with three broad planks on each side. Existing alongside these simple boats are craft the same size of much more sophisticated construction. They have six narrow strakes on either side of the keel plank and well curved sections like those of the *patam* and the *daurat nauka.* Like these latter boats, and unlike the majority of the smooth skinned river boats, almost all the clinker built boats are identical in form at bow and stern.

Although the shape is the same at either end, the run of the planking in the bow and stern sometimes differs. The planking at the bow follows the pattern of the smooth skinned boats. At the stern the planks are sometimes tapered and all brought to the keel plank, or to the garboard strakes, which are sometimes not tapered.

On all the *digkata* boats examined, the garboard strakes were joined to the keel plank either with a European style clinker seam or with a diagonal join which, in some cases at least, was a clinker seam much bevelled away. One boat examined while she was being built was about 40ft long, fastened with short galvanised iron nails with in addition boatbuilder's staples fastened in slots cut very deep into the clinker planking at intervals of about 6in. Her builder said that ordinary nails were not so strong as boatbuilder's staples but they involved less labour in the fastenings. He said that in a bigger boat they would be essential for strength. The boat was to have deck beams, and then one further narrow horizontal whale. The general form and construction of her lower hull was similar in some ways to that of the ancient Graveney boat, discovered near Faversham in Kent in late 1970 and now under conservation in the National Maritime Museum.

Some of the largest of these clinker built craft are among the finest of all the river boats of East Pakistan. One large boat about 50ft long (page 87) was built entirely of continuous hardwood planks 2in thick. She was fastened entirely with boatbuilder's staples, both inside and out, which were set in deep slots cut in the clinker planking. Each plank was rabbeted for a quarter of its thickness, so that at the overlap the planking was 3 instead of 4in thick. The sharp projecting edges of the planks were smoothed off. The garboard strakes were fastened to the keel plank with a very shallow diagonal join. Even for this seam boat-builder's staples were used. The framing was entirely orthodox, with *baka*, *gocha* and *kunia* entirely separate from one another. The outer faces of the frames were roughly notched to fit the

17 The stern of a round-hulled boat from Khulna district

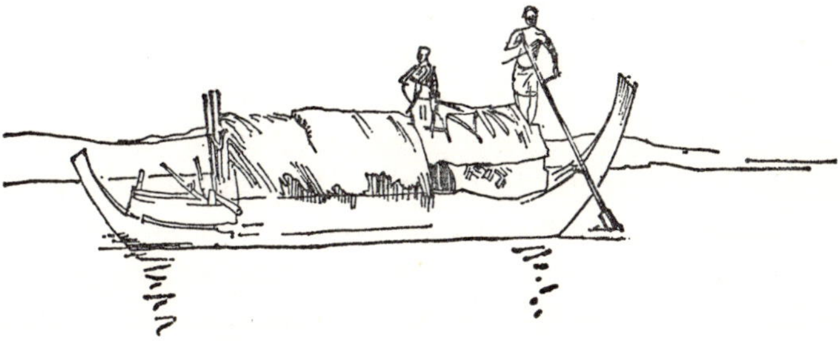

18 A boat from Khulna with curved *golois*

clinker construction. At places where the gap would otherwise have been considerable the frames had been fully notched.

She was a shallow boat. Her full depth was only 3½ft though her beam was 12ft. Her *golois*, which were turned up more than 45° to the horizontal, were continuous with her massive keel plank. She was entirely covered with a great *chauni* of woven bamboo, like the tilt of an American pioneer's wagon. She had walkways built on the ends of her deck beams where they projected through the hull on either side. Her crew walked on these when they poled her in shallow streams. She appeared to make no water at all and she had brought a cargo of cement dry all the way from Sylhet to Dacca.

Besides this series of clinker built boats of Sylhet there are other places in East Pakistan where clinker construction, with the seams the reverse of the European style, occurs.

South of Khulna on the Pussur River is an area where the local *dinghys* are clinker built. Two different types of boat are in use here. One is about 12ft long, very lightly built of ½in planking, with the keel plank extending at either end into flat *golois*. There are four planks on each side varying in breadth from 4 to more than 6in. They differ from the Sylhet boats in that the keel plank is curved up more steeply in the stern than in the bow, so that the after sections of the boat are fuller. In reverse of the planking pattern sometimes adopted in the Sylhet boats, the planking is tapered out to the keel plank at the bow, but brought up at the stern so that the plank ends form the actual gunwhale of the boat. These plank ends are not rounded off, so that the gunwhale at the stern has a characteristically serrated appearance. These boats, which are used by cultivators to travel to their work in fields by the waterside, have neither frames nor thwarts. They are of extremely light and fragile appearance and they are usually paddled by one man sitting in the extreme stern.

The second type of Khulna *digkata* boat is larger, from 15 to 20ft long, more heavily built, with only three strakes, 9in or 1ft in breadth and 1in thick on either side. They are used for general watermen's work.

Page 105 (*above*) Sea-going boats, some of them over 60ft long, 7ft deep and 12 or 14ft in the beam, big sewn *balams* like this one are quite without iron in the whole of their structure; (*below*) her six oars at rest, a big *balam*, deep laden, under sail in the Bay of Bengal

Page 106 (*above*) A big *sampan* be
ing to windward; (*right*) stern of
kotia in Karachi harbour

In Mymensingh district, in the western part near the Brahmaputra, we saw another kind of clinker built boat. These were small *dinghys*, of entirely orthodox shape with the stern *goloi* slightly higher than that at the bow, but with the planks, both the main planking and the horizontal whales, laid in the East Pakistan clinker way. In this they differed from the Sylhet boats for the horizontal whales of these are laid edge to edge. Apart from the seams these clinker built *dinghys* of Mymensingh were indistinguishable from smooth skinned river boats.

In Dacca district near Mograpara Hat I saw a group of small *dinghys* which looked as if they might be clinker built, but I was not able to examine them closely.

Rahman told us that he could remember as recently as 1920 small *dinghys* were being built in Noakhali with the planks laid in European clinker fashion. They were fastened with pins of split bamboo driven into holes slightly smaller in diameter than the pins themselves. The pins were charred to soften their outer surfaces before they were driven home. Rahman told me that these boats had been immensely strong and had sometimes lasted for forty or fifty years instead of the fifteen or so years which is the average life of a smooth skinned boat. Rahman called them *khil nauka*, which literally means 'pin boats'.

Class 3: The clinker built boats of the Upper Ganges

In *Water Transport*, James Hornell made several references to the existence on the Upper Ganges, in Bihar and what was then called the United Provinces, of a series of large clinker built boats constructed in European style. He described them in his various writings as 'vessels of much the same general hull design as the *pulwar* (that is, as the smooth skinned river boats described above) but differing in being built of overlapping planks'. He gave them names, *patela*, *melni* and *ulakh* and said (inaccurately I fear in the light of what we saw in Sylhet and Mymensingh and Khulna) that they represented 'the extraordinary and isolated presence of a clinker built type' in Southern Asia.

Although from time to time many boats from the Upper Ganges do trade down into East Pakistan, even by the early 1950s boats of the clinker built type had become very rare visitors. In all our travels on the big rivers we saw only one. She was anchored with a group of her smooth skinned sisters on the Meghna below Chandpur and we saw her only very briefly from a steamer as we swept by. But from the men of smooth skinned boats from Bihar and Uttar Pradesh we heard something of the clinker built boats from the same region.

These men recognised the clinker built boats as soon as they were described. They knew them as *patalias* and the information provided by several different boatmen suggests that the *patalia* may be a dying type. It was spoken of by the crew of one big Indian boat as the ancient boat of the Ganges, and was described as being of quite different construction from the smooth skinned river boats. They were said to have a flat bottom built of two layers of heavy planking, one running fore and aft and the other athwartship, fastened together with iron spikes. This floor was forced up in bow and stern and on to it were built sides of very heavy narrow planks laid European clinker fashion. In the bigger boats the overlaps of thick planks were so deep that the sides were actually three planks thick. They had no *baka*, but numerous *kunia* and *gocha* which extended from the chine to the bulwark up the clinker built sides.

These boats were dying out, the boatmen said, because they were difficult to repair; because the chine was a weak point in their construction; because their massive sides made them heavy for their size and reduced the amount of cargo they could carry; and because, although they were simpler to build than round bilged boats fastened with boatbuilder's staples, they needed much more timber and in the end were more expensive. Another possible cause of their falling out of use is that they were built of costly straight runs of narrow planking and did not lend themselves to the use of short lengths of timber in the way the smooth skinned form of construction does.

Many smooth skinned river boats from Bihar and Uttar Pradesh which come down into East Pakistan are equipped with small tenders, about 18ft long, which are built in the manner ascribed to the *patalia.* They have flat bottoms of planks fastened together nowadays with boatbuilder's staples. Above the chine are three or four massive strakes of thick planking fastened European clinker fashion with spikes with large flat heads. Above the uppermost of these are a couple of planks laid *binekata* fashion and fastened with boatbuilder's staples. The boats are double ended with stem and sternpost and have tiny vestigial *golois.* They have a few *baka* and regularly spaced *gocha.*

A Pakistani friend showed us a strange little boat which had evidently been built for pleasure purposes many years before. Nobody knew when she was built or where she had come from. She had a flat bottom, massive sides planked European clinker fashion, and fastened with iron spikes, many *kunia* and some *gocha* but no *baka.* She had a transom stern.

Class 4: The chine built smooth skinned boats of Dacca district

These are small cargo boats which at first glance appeared to be ordinary smooth skinned vessels. In fact they were flat bottomed with a hard chine like the *patalias* but with the planks joined with boatbuilder's staples, edge to edge in the normal way. They had flat shovel shaped *golois* which, of course, served no purpose at all in a boat constructed in this fashion. They steered with fixed, semi-balanced steering oars, which despite the small size of the boats were for steering only and not for propulsion. They looked in every way like the result of an attempt by some outside agency to produce a useful type of boat for the smaller rivers which made use of the traditional building methods and materials and was near enough to the traditional form to be readily acceptable to the boatmen, and yet which would be cheaper to construct. Perhaps that is exactly what they were. No opportunity occurred to investigate their origins or to examine one closely. We saw them nowhere but in the Dacca district.

Class 5: Flat-bottomed boats.

There is a type of small flat-bottomed boat much used around Dacca and Narayanganj, but also seen elsewhere in East Pakistan which is locally known as a *korsha.* I am told that the name comes from a Bengali word for a small votive vessel used in Hindu temples which is of similar shape to these little boats. They are double ended, often without sheer, but some with the flat bottom steeply canted up at either end, giving the boat a marked sheer and an appearance distinctly like the big sea-going dories of St Pierre in the Gulf of St Lawrence. The *korsha* is fastened with boatbuilder's staples and the planks of her bottom run fore and aft. She is rarely more than 20ft long and she resembles no other kind of boat in East Pakistan. *Korshas* are much used for fishing and ferrying and occasionally, fitted with a *chauni*, as small cargo carriers. A very similar type of boat is sometimes carried by the big cargo vessels from Bihar and Uttar Pradesh. The crew of one such boat said they had bought their *korsha* in Assam, and that they regarded her as an Assamese type of boat. We did not ourselves see *korshas* in our own travels in Assam, but these were limited in range. The existence of the dory-like *korsha* with its wide planks and chine construction, all its timber hand sawn, would seem to cast doubt on the theory, recently expressed in America, that such boats developed only where power saw mills were available.

Class 6: Dugouts

Dugouts of various kinds occur in many parts of East Pakistan. In addition to the dugout-based clinker built boats of the Khasi and Jantia hill valleys we saw heavy flat-sheered dugouts with square punt-like ends in the wild valleys that lead out of the Garo hills down into Pakistan from a remote and inaccessible part of India. In every district of East Pakistan which is subject to the annual inundation the Palmyra palm dugout of the type illustrated in James Hornell's *Water Transport* is used, but singly, rather than in the coupled pairs shown by Hornell, and the *dongha*, as these dugouts are usually called in East Pakistan, are smaller than those shown by Hornell and usually flat-sheered. In this bulb-shaped craft, the trunk end sealed with a mud wall or a fragment of the palm's soft interior, the cultivator poles himself between paddy and jute fields, or even from house to house in a flooded homestead.

But it is in the extreme south-east of Pakistan on the rivers of Noakhali and Chittagong, that the sewn, plank-extended dugout reaches what is perhaps its most highly developed form in the world today. These plank-extended dugouts and the simpler forms from which they have developed and which still continue alongside them are not strictly river boats, because they sail across the open Bay of Bengal from the Chittagong coast to the towns and villages of the delta. And now that the boat business is booming with the development of East Pakistan and the general increase in economic activity which is taking place, they trade regularly far inland to Dacca and to the north. But they should strictly be described with the sea boats of East Pakistan.

SEA BOATS

The sea boats can be divided by the systems on which they are built into three classes:

Class 1: Dugouts and plank-extended dugouts

The cargo-carrying dugouts are known by the general term *saranga*, the largest of them as *kuda.* They are cut from single logs, hollowed out until only the equivalent of a thin planking, 1in or 1½in thick in the largest craft, which may be 60-70ft long, is left. The hollowing is done with fire and adze. Before the hollowing is far advanced shallow holes are drilled from the outside of the log to the depth the planking is required to take. The hollowing process stops when the inside ends of the holes are reached and the holes are sealed with wooden plugs. Dozens of these holes pock mark the outside of a big *saranga.*

The ends of the log are left solid, shaped in a characteristic rounded tapering form very reminiscent of some kinds of *goloi* in appearance. The dugout is then expanded; after the softening with fire its sides are forced apart, and in consequence it acquires, as every expanded dugout must, a low gently curved sheer, and the ends rise to form low overhangs. To keep the sides from closing up again the *saranga* are fitted with very solid floor timbers which nowadays are usually secured with iron spikes. When the hulls become damaged or worn they are repaired with planks fastened with boatbuilder's staples. As the hulls are often heavily tarred it is often difficult to tell with an old *saranga* how much dugout survives and how much has been replaced with planks. *Sarangas* are usually covered with a *chauni* throughout their length. They have a light mast stepped at the bow and a single squaresail.

Many small dugouts built in this fashion are used in south-eastern districts for fishing, ferrying and general waterman's work. They are light, graceful craft and their appearance belies completely any idea that a dugout must necessarily be a heavy or unseaworthy vessel. Their shells are often thinner and lighter than those of plank-built boats of similar size and form. Many of them have their solid ends left in flat board-like *golois* like some of the smaller and simpler plank-built boats of the Sylhet district and the larger, often frameless, *daurat nauka*. They closely resemble these plank-built boats in general appearance and it is sometimes only by very close examination (especially when they have been much repaired) that one can establish that they are of dugout construction. They tend to need more floors to keep them in shape than the plank-built boats do, and these floors extend up the sides into continuous futtocks.

Some of these small dugouts are extended with plank sides to make a graceful and able type of canoe which is used for sea fishing. The basic expanded dugout with its irregularly spaced sawn floors is pierced down the gunwale at intervals of about 6in. A 1in plank which has been shaped very slightly is then held in position with clamps for a few feet down the gunwale. It is drilled at intervals corresponding with the holes in the dugout and lashed into position with one or two turns of split bamboo through a few of the paired holes (page 88). The seam between plank and dugout is then caulked with teased-out old rope and the whole packed on both sides with a seal of grey mud. Over this mud strips of the broad green leaves of palms are laid, and over these in turn tightly bunched long coarse grasses. On the outside of the boat the whole seam is finished off with a protecting cover of split bamboo strips. The whole is held in position, and plank and dugout held together, with a tight sewing of split bamboo, the stitch crossed diagonally between the paired holes inside the boat, but not on the outside. The holes are then finally plugged and the bamboo stitching, jammed so that it will work as little as possible, with teased-out old rope—driven in hard.

To support the side planks, as the builders put it, 'against the blows of the sea', half a dozen short round spars, often roughly cut and still with the bark on them, are bound tightly into position with their feet against the side of the dugout just below the seam inside. Over these, and at the level of the seam, two bamboo stringers are lashed into place with split bamboo binding, which is passed through the seam holes at intervals of about 2ft. The vertical and the horizontal spars are not lashed to one another. The heads of the vertical spars are secured to the upper edge of the plank by lashings passed through holes drilled in the plank. Occasionally a narrow second plank is added, nailed roughly into position.

The largest of these sewn fishing canoes which I examined measured 32ft by 6ft 2in by 3ft. They are dismantled each year when the great seas of the south-west monsoon make sea fishing impossible, and the basic dugout is used as a river fishing boat. In November, at the beginning of the cooler, calmer weather the planks are sewn on again and the boat, equipped with a spritsail but propelled mainly with paddles, goes back to use in the open sea. I was told that a well-made dugout will last twenty years of this work, but towards the end of that time so many pieces of timber will have been used to repair her that she has become almost a plank-built boat.

The method used in building these small fishing canoes has been described at length because just the same principles are used in constructing the great cargo carrying *balams* which are no more than greatly enlarged versions of the simple canoe, both in their general shape and in the way they are built.

The *Chittagong Gazetteer* defines four types of cargo-carrying plank-extended dugout, the *ad balam* with one plank each side, the *balam* proper with two planks a side, the *gadu*, which has three planks a side, and needs thirteen men to work her, and the *jalyanao* with four planks a side. The *Gazetteer* adds that the *jalyanao* is used for deep-sea fishing. In my experience the word *balam* was used indiscriminately by the boatmen to describe all three types and the number of planks depends more on what timber is available than upon the size of the vessel. Moreover, a *balam* does not always have the same number of planks on each side. The greatest number of planks a side I saw was five, and the *balams* concerned, which were between 60 and 70ft long, were not of the very largest kind.

These large sewn *balams* are wonderful and impressive vessels. Sea-going boats, some of them over 60ft long, 7ft deep and 12-14ft in the beam, they are quite without iron in their whole structure (page 105). The vertical, partly balanced rudder, works in loops of hand-twisted jute rope. The occasional beams are lashed into position with split bamboo, which is the main form of fastening throughout the vessel. The heavy floors which keep the expanded dugout base in shape are, in *balams* built in the classic tradition, secured with treenails. Above the turn of the bilge the framing is a complex of light vertical spars and stringers. As in the little canoes the vertical and horizontal spars of this framing are separately lashed to the planking and they are not secured to each other. This framing provides a strong but flexible stiffening to the planking which can work in a moderate sea without coming to any harm. There are no fixed decks and the crew of up to fourteen men live on top of the cargo under the bamboo *chauni* and row the boat from loose planks laid in the bow.

At the after end of this temporary foredeck is stepped the mast, usually in a tabernacle made from a heavy log with a deep notch cut into it. From a yard on this mast the single squaresail is set. The *balam* is a sea-going boat, and her rigging is stouter and more complex than that of the river boats. She has numerous shrouds and backstays and a forestay. With her long narrow hull and well-cut sail the *balam* can make some sort of a showing to windward in the expert hands of a good crew. I once saw one with a long, thin spar, probably a bamboo pole, its foot secured in the bulwarks to windward slightly abaft the mast, its head thrusting forward the luff of the squaresail about a third of the way down from the head, much in the way the 'vargord' used to be used in Cornish luggers more than a century ago, before the introduction of the high peaked lug with a short luff made their use unnecessary. Some Viking ships were equipped with a similar device, the *beiti-ass*, the tacking spar. *Skuldelev I,* the big cargo ship, the *Knarr* type, now restored at Roskilde in Denmark, was fitted with a tacking spar. Many *balams* carry a short second mast from which a lateen sail of the type used in sea boats of Class 3 (which is described below) is set. This second sail no doubt helps them a great deal in sailing to windward. *Balams* so rigged have a distinctly medieval appearance under sail.

The planked dugout canoes end at bow and stern in a tall tapering board which occupies the space between the plank ends above the flat top of the *goloi*-like end of the dugout. Many big *balams* have bow and stern shaped in the same way—the board shows clearly in the photographs of balams in this book (page 105). Others have shaped stem and sternposts of heavy timber lashed into place instead of this board. I have even seen one sewn *balam* with a clipper bow, complete with trail boards. There is also a type of sewn boat, locally called a *murina*, and constructed in the same way as a sewn *balam*, which has pointed ends, the stern rising to a rounded head ornament. *Murinas* are much used for lightering cargo at Chittagong port.

The sewn *balam* persisted in large numbers in the mid-twentieth century. She had certain advantages, perhaps, of flexibility, ease of repair and economy of heavy frame timbers, over iron-fastened boats. In one single convoy of eight of these floating coelacanths, each laden with firewood, we met once in the river system just east of Barisal town, seven were big, sewn boats of different forms. But in recent years the metal-fastened *balam* has become much more common than the sewn boat, at least in the more accessible areas of the south-east. The metal-fastened *balam* is in her simplest form a close imitation of the sewn boat. I have never seen one of these metal-fastened *balams* under construction, but according to their crews their planks are half rabbeted like the planks of the smooth skinned river boats and fastened with spikes driven diagonally downwards across the seams. Certainly boatbuilder's staples are not used and certainly the light side frames, with their network of stringers running fore and aft and quite separate from the heavy floor timbers of the basic dugout, are of the inserted kind.

The additional strength provided by iron fastenings and the development of a technique of using numerous narrow planks in place of a few very broad ones has resulted in the development of variations in the shape of metal-fastened *balams*. Almost all the larger ones now have a graceful sheer with the stern markedly higher than the bow. The sloping boards at bow and stern tend to become smaller and the general appearance to become closer to that of the round-hulled river boats. In some new boats the dugout base has disappeared altogether and has been replaced by a plank-built structure of the same form. Thus the history of the *balam* tends to parallel the history of the clinker built boat in northern Europe which went through a development process also involving the use of iron fastenings and more and narrower planks.

I saw one vessel in which the influence of the round-hulled river boats seemed to be so great that she represented a combination of the characteristics of both types of craft. Her profile was that of a big *balam*, but she was beamier and shallower than any other *balam* I saw. She was plank built throughout and fastened with boatbuilder's staples. Her planking did not run from bow to stern like that of a *balam*, but was laid like that of a river boat with a basic spoon of planks running up into the sheer and heavy whales running the length of the vessel above. Built into her bow and stern were shaped blocks of solid timber like the shaped ends of a basic dugout. Her framing was of the orthodox river boat type. She was beautifully finished. The four bollards which many *balams* have in the bows were carved and decorated pieces of finished timber. Her mast tabernacle was carved and decorated and the lines of her frames picked out in big-headed nails. She steered with an oar the carved head of the loom of which must have been 30ft above the water.

Metal-fastened *balams* steer either with semi-balanced rudders on the quarter or with these great oars, which, unlike the steering oars of the river boats, are little used for propulsion. They are longer and heavier than the river boats' oars, for the long, straight *balam* needs a more powerful steering mechanism than the shallow, beamy river boats. The steering oars are controlled by a rope traveller on a cross-bar between two upright posts and their movement restricted.

The big *balam* is a powerful and attractive type of boat, and her appearance is further enhanced by the brilliant decoration with which many *balams* are embellished. Some of these great-plank-extended dugouts are among the world's most vividly painted boats. Bow and stern are picked out in a pattern of triangles and rectangles in green and white, red and orange, while the tapering bow and stern boards are covered with complex designs of every kind (page 105). Often oculi are slipped into the pattern, either as a pair of mammal-like eyes on the end boards themselves, or low down on the dugout part of the hull, so that they are under water when the vessel is deep laden. Down the length of the boat white circles 1ft in diameter with green and orange centres pick out the sheer. Even the roughly finished masts are sometimes decorated with bands of bright paint.

Class 2: The Chittagong sampans

The most common boat of the south-east coast of Pakistan is the *sampan*, a vessel of completely different form from any of those so far described. She is a short, high-sided vessel and her general form, particularly her high transom stern with the twin horns rising above it, suggests Chinese influence. She has hard chines and, though her bottom has a marked rise fore and aft she can sit bolt upright on the mud. She has a high vertical stem. *Sampans* are the only boats in East Pakistan to have hatch coamings and fixed decks nailed to deck beams. They steer with stern rudders (page 106).

They are built on a quite different system from any of the other boats. The bottom is first assembled from planks laid edge to edge without rabbeting and fastened with nails driven in at right angles to the seam from triangular-shaped notches cut into one of the planks. The same system of edge joining is used in the construction in Japan of beach boats and larger craft up to a considerable size. In them, and in the Chittagong *sampans*, the nail notches are subsequently plugged with wooden chips. Next, the floor frames are nailed to the bottom boards and the side planks above the hard chine are built up, edge joined in the same way as the bottom planks. The side frames are then inserted and the deck beams are fitted. Finally the deck planks are laid without edge joining.

Sampans can be divided by size into roughly four groups. The smallest are the open *sampans*, 14-16ft long, rowed by one man standing in the stern facing forward and rowing with the looms of the oars crossed in front of him. I have seen boatmen on a Swiss lake rowing in exactly the same fashion. The small *sampan* carries a boomed spritsail with a very high cut foot. I have never seen one trying to work to windward. They are used for general watermen's work.

The next size of *sampan* is 16-18ft long. She is steered from a well aft which is really the after part of the open boat. Forward of this well a hatch is built up for cargo. She carries the same kind of spritsail as the smallest *sampans*.

The smallest decked *sampans* are 20-30ft long, and the largest class are high-sided boxy looking vessels 35ft long by 8ft deep and 12-15ft broad. These larger *sampans* set a kind of lateen sail. The long flexible yard is nearly vertical in the part that lies forward of the mast. The sail is really a settee, because the foot is in two parts, with a vestigial luff in front of the mast and a vestigal tack line holding down a point on the foot of the sail at the mast. The after part of the sail is boomed with a boom secured to the mast with a rope sling.

The mast is stepped in a tabernacle of the kind used in *balams* and is supported by a forest of shrouds and backstays. *Sampans* of the two larger kinds regularly work to windward when deep laden (page 106). The yard and sail are invariably carried on the port side of the mast and when on the port tack the sail bellies back against the mast like a standing lug. *Sampans* usually have to be rowed round to go about. In light airs I have seen a big *sampan* with a jib set from the spare yard, the end of which was pressed into use as a bowsprit.

When the wind fails, four or six men row the *sampan* from a standing position on the foredeck. Because these vessels are high sided they have to row short deep strokes with long oars.

Big *sampans* venture far afield. Flying over the Bay of Bengal in the cold weather they are to be seen in their dozens sailing up and down the coast. With the big *balams* they sail as far north as Dacca and to the Indian border in the west and they are said to work far down the coast of Burma. Their crews live on the after deck under a hood of woven bamboo. Their bedrolls and their few possessions are stowed under the after bench which runs across the transom. They sleep stretched out on the polished boards. Their food is cooked on an open fire on the foredeck.

Class 3: Carvel built boats

Because they are of the familiar, orthodox European and American skeleton construction a description of the hulls of these vessels, which are known in Chittagong simply as 'boats' (as opposed to *balams* and *sampans*), is less important than their interesting rig. It is likely that vessels of this type have been in use for a very long time on the Hooghli as well as the Karnafuli and that they came here with the British and have been modified under outside influence from time to time.

These boats are the Bermuda rigged ketches which we so often saw on the rivers of the delta beating across the broad streams, their sails, always very white, standing out in such contrast with the squaresails of the river boats. To the foreign hulls has been adopted a variation of the Arab lateen rig. The masts are actually short and stubby and stayed like the masts of an ordinary gaff ketch. Far above the top of the mast towers the pliant vertical spar of a lateen yard to which is laced the luff of a lateen sail, the foot and back of which have been so cut that the foot comes parallel with the deck and can be extended by a boom. The sail is not what a nineteenth-century yachtsman would have called a sliding gunter lug, the yard does not slide up and down the mast. There is no reefing system. To take in sail the great yard is lowered down on deck, the sail is made fast and the whole hauled up again to get them out of the way. Thus the boatmen of Chittagong have, probably within the last hundred years, developed for themselves a sail which has all the advantages of the Bermudan (and it is in a fairly advanced form too, for the sail is of high aspect ratio, with a short foot) with none of the difficulties of staying and mast making which go with the sail in its contemporary American and European form. Of course, the long yard tends to whip about at the tip, but that can be an advantage in a climate where extreme variations of wind strength can happen in a few seconds with no warning to speak of.

These tall triangular sails are reminiscent of the Bermudan rigged trading schooners I saw some years ago off the island of Ruad on the coast of Syria. With them the mast and yard were all in one piece, but the masts were stayed like gaff rigged masts, with a great length of flexible spar above the shrouds. These schooners, for all their handsome appearance, looked brutes to sail and their huge sails most difficult to handle. And yet they have been sailing for as long as anybody has been able to trace back, and they make money, even in the modern world.

I suspect that the Bermudan sail developed quite independently at a number of different places and periods. It grew up on Chesapeake Bay, in Bermuda itself, in the eastern Mediterranean, perhaps much earlier in the East Indies, from where it may have spread to Holland. Perhaps it grew up and died away again in other parts of the world as well, and has never been noticed. In small craft there would seem to be only one stage, the lateen mast is scrapped and the heel of the yard stepped in its place. Something like that seems to have happened on the east coast of the United States. With bigger vessels there were clearly two stages. First the foot of the yard was brought to the foot of the mast, so that the yard stuck up vertically. This is the stage at Chittagong. Then the mast itself was done away with, as in the Syrian schooners today.

The 'boats' of Chittagong are something of a proving ground for different rigs. Some have an ordinary lateen sail on the mainmast and a sail of the type just described on the mizzen. A number of them are rigged with two Chinese lugs, the mast nearer the stern being the larger of the two. These sails, the general appearance and characteristics of which are exactly those of the sail of *Jester* which H. G. Hasler sailed in the single handed trans-Atlantic race of 1960, seem to suit the sharp round hull form. Certainly boats rigged in this way look very well indeed among the square sailed boats on the big rivers. This sail, like the Chinese hulls and oars of the *sampans*, must have come creeping up the coast from Burma and Malaya many hundreds of years ago.

Conclusions

The Chittagong 'boat', the *balam*, the *saranga*, the *sampan* are all self evident types in very different stages of development. The *saranga* is right at the beginning, the *sampan* extremely sophisticated and mature. The very uniformity of construction of all the numerous different types of smooth skinned river boats, the *binekata*, suggests, strongly, a common origin, and the great differences of hull form suggest that that origin was a long way back. The Sylhet *digkata* boats show beyond doubt that a clinker or lapstrake form of construction can come into existence quite spontaneously from the desire to extend a hollowed out log, just as the smooth skinned boat is known to have done in some cases in different parts of the world. The *balam* shows that it has done so quite independently in East Pakistan.

Of all man's artefacts, boats by their very nature are likely to spread the influence of their builders furthest and most often. There are many influences at work from all over the world in almost any community of watermen with access to the open sea, particularly the seas of Asia, which, compared with the seas of Europe and America, are relatively easy to sail. It is therefore important to point out that the suggestions that follow are necessarily tentative.

It is not inconceivable that clinker form of build grew up in the gorges of the Khasi and Jantia Hills because the timbers available there, which include pine, were of a quality to shrink and warp more easily than the hardwoods available elsewhere. They did not therefore make for good permanently watertight joints edge to edge, and an overlap grew up instead. The rabbets of the seams of the *binekata* boats may themselves be vestigial overlaps and indicate a clinker origin for by far the greatest number of the boats of East Pakistan. Certainly, from their variety, the *binekata* boats are very old.

European and American writers sometimes write as if the 'normal' way of building a boat was to nail planks, not joined edge to edge, around a backbone of pre-erected and pre-shaped frames, and as if the only permissible variation from this was to build in clinker style. But in East Pakistan all the boats described, except the one type of Chittagong vessel, are built of planks joined edge to edge with the frames inserted and shaped afterwards. The people there all think of a boat as a shell with strengthening frames, not as a skeleton with a skin stretched around it. To the builder of the Sylhet canoe and the Chittagong *sampan* alike, though the boats are thousands of years apart in development, the continuity of the outer fabric of the hull is all important. They must build a floating vessel, which may or may not be strength-

Page 123 (*above*) A *bheddi* is a short keeled boat with a long overhanging bow and a sloping transom stern; (*below*) *charts* discharging firewood at low tide

Page 124 (*above*) A double balance board and outrigger fitted *ekdar hora*; (*below*) a big *ekdar hora* sailing fast in a monsoon breeze. Her whole crew, including the helmsman, who is steering with the yoke and lines visible in the photograph, are out on the balance boards behind the sail and there is no one in the boat herself at all

ened by ribs which take their shape from the vessel into which they are fitted, not vice versa. From my own observations, slight as they have been, in Asia between the Mediterranean coast and the coasts of Japan, I have formed the view that perhaps the majority of the world's boatbuilders have thought of a boat as a shell with strengthening frames and not as a skeleton with skin on it, and have built boats that way. Certainly skeleton construction is much newer and less widespread than writers on the history of the boat used to suppose.

There seems little doubt but that the *binekata* boats like the *digkata* represent an evolutionary pattern from the expanded and extended dugout, although the surviving series is neither so simple or so complete. The *goloi* is so similar to the solid end of a dugout. The sheer of so many boats is close to that automatically assumed by an expanded dugout. The existence of frameless plank built boats, the distribution of frames in those that have them, which suggests descent from frames like those of the sewn fishing canoes of Chittagong, all these factors are overwhelming evidence of the dugout origin of the *binekata* as of the *digkata*.

Like the Scandinavian ships found in bogs, burial moulds and under the sea, but even more so, the different types of *binekata* and *digkata* boats illustrate in great detail the history of their construction. Contemporary thought ascribes also to this other great ship family a descent from expanded, extended dugouts. Other parallels are obvious. The different relative shapes and proportions of a *ghashi* and a *pallar*, structurally identical, compare with those of a longship and a *knarr*. The change in the run of the planking below the topside whales is as distinct as the change at the fifth strake in *Skuldelev I* or at the *meginhufr* of the Oseberg ship, and could arise from similar circumstances of development. There are parallels with other north European ship types. The *patalia* structurally has features in common with the *kogge*. Reverse clinker has been known in Europe at least since the Bruges boat of the fifth-sixth century AD.

Six

THE STORY OF THE STEAMERS

In the entrance hall of my house on the outskirts of Dacca there hung a heavy brass bell. Its walls were at least half an inch thick, although the bell was only about a foot high, so it sounded a deep rich note, rather like the sonorous warning of a bell buoy, when it was struck with the heavy iron clapper. From this clapper hung a short lanyard with a fancy knot at the lower end, just the right height to clasp, and very tempting to children, so that when a family was visiting us the house was often filled with the deep note of the bell, followed by shrieks of delight and a noise of scampering feet.

On the side of the bell was engraved in bold capitals, filled in with bright red paint, the inscription *Nowgong 1881.* Nowgong is a district in Upper Assam, far up the Brahmaputra, in the comparatively narrow valley between the mountains of Assam and the foothills of the Himalayas. The *Nowgong*, whose long life was tolled out to the strokes of this bell, was a small side paddle steamer of about 150 tons, built by the India General Steam Navigation Company at their shipyard at Nos 6 and 7 Garden Reach, Calcutta, in 1881. She was designed to be a line steamer for use on the smaller rivers of the Brahmaputra—Ganges system, carrying 175-250 passengers (in very cramped quarters), besides a few tons of cargo.

Her great days were during the opening of the mail service to middle Assam, where tea gardens, including many of those now in East Pakistan, were being opened up in the 1890s. This service ran up the narrowing valley of the Surma River to the feet of the high hills. The small size and shallow draft of the *Nowgong* made her particularly suitable for the narrow, twisting upper reaches of the Surma. Ten years later, when the railway network was gradually creeping over East Pakistan, the mails went by train and the steamers took to carrying bulk cargo. The *Nowgong* and some other ships were refitted with new compound engines of greatly increased power, making them into towing steamers. They worked up the Surma with small barges lashed alongside them, making fast voyages which earned big dividends. After this work the *Nowgong* went back to passenger and cargo carrying in the smaller rivers and she worked at this for fifty more years.

The story of the river steamer fleets of the Brahmaputra and the Ganges has a special romance of its own. What the steamers on the Mississippi and the Hudson, Lake Champlain and the St Lawrence were to the United States and Canada, the side-wheeler with two 600 ton barges lashed one on either side has been to the history of the country north of the Bay of Bengal. The history of American steam boats is quite well recorded, but little or nothing has been written about the steamers of these great eastern rivers. Yet it is doubtful if the British would be the heirs to a taste for morning and afternoon tea if there had been no steamers on the Brahmaputra. The tea gardens of Assam could never have been started without them, and without the tea gardens of Assam it is unlikely that tea would have been so cheap and plentiful in England as to become a national habit. And without the steamers to bring it out of the monsoon country where it grows, jute fibre could never have become the cheapest and most adaptable natural fibre and the basis of a large industry.

In 1824 Bengal businessmen and others, alive to the possible advantages of shortening the four months' voyage which separated them from European markets, raised a public subscription of £8,000 as a bonus to the first vessel which should steam out from England and back again twice within a stipulated time. The *Enterprise*, built at Deptford in 1824, tried for the prize a year later and made the passage in 113 days. In the words of a contemporary press account:

> The steam-vessel called the *Enterprise* has left the banks of the Thames for those of the Ganges. Her burden is 500 tons. She has two sixty-horse-power engines. The boilers, which are made of copper, extend across the ship, with seven furnaces, each seven feet in depth. Although the *Enterprise* will make use of her sails when the wind permits, she will rely principally on her steam, and for this purpose she must necessarily take out three hundred tons of coals. The coals are partly contained in chambers, within the sides of the vessel, covered with sheet iron, and partly in tanks beneath; which, as they are emptied of coals, will be filled with water to keep the vessel properly ballasted. The cabins, of which there are twenty, are furnished with every convenience.

She took too long to earn the bonus, but she is supposed to have steamed for 62 out of her 100 days at sea and at full speed in fine weather she could, according to some authorities, make 6-7 knots —which after all was still the best speed of some tramp steamers 100 years later. Her captain was paid half the bonus, and the ship was bought by the government to trade between Calcutta and Singapore.

Nine years later, by which time steamboats were becoming well established on the inland waterways of North America and on the coasts of Britain, a regular commercial steamer service was established on thc Ganges by the East India Company and soon there were four vessels trading on the river. They were peculiar looking little ships, side paddle steamers, each with a tall thin funnel and a single mast with two squaresails, like those of a river sailing boat. They carried cargo and crew only. Each steamer towed a sailing barge as big as herself, rigged with two masts with squaresails and spritsails. In the barge, which was called the 'accommodation boat', there were cabins where the passengers lived, but they ate at the captain's table on board the steamer and to move from one vessel to the other they had to negotiate a gangway.

The accommodation boats were fitted with four first-class cabins, each measuring 12ft by 8ft, with bunks for two people who were charged 300 rupees each for the privilege of a passage from Calcutta to Allahabad. In addition the passengers had to pay a messing charge of 4 rupees a day to the captain, and this gentleman made more out of the messing than he did from his pay. It took 22-28 days to get to Allahabad, depending on how much water was going down the Ganges. Long as it seems, this was a great improvement on any method of travelling which had ever existed in the whole of history in India before, and the service was deservedly popular. Bookings had to be made a month in advance and the whole of the passage money deposited at the same time.

True to the traditions of the East India Company, quasi-naval discipline was maintained in those early river steamers. They carried guns, and there were strict rules for servants. 'Servants', said the regulations, 'are required to be always clean and dressed with their turbands. European or Christian servants are never permitted to appear without their jacket and shoes; they are required to keep their hair cut and are not permitted to wear it long and brushy. Each servant, when attending table, is required to carry a clean napkin in his hands.'

The river steamers, and the East India Company's tug boats which towed the great East Indiamen and other ships from the sea up the difficult Hooghli river to Calcutta, proved profitable enough that private enterprise took up steam. In 1837 a 'Steam Tug Association' was founded in Calcutta and from it grew the India General Steam Navigation Company, which was established in 1844. The new company's prospectus stated clearly what it was setting out to do.

'Whereas at a public meeting of merchants, capitalists, inhabitants, and others, holden in Calcutta on the 6th day of February, 1844, the following gentlemen, that is to say, Albert de Hochepied Larpent, Samuel Smith, John Allan, Radhamadhub Bonnerj Rustumjee Cowasjee, Alexander Rogers, John Storm and A. Thompson, with power to add to their number, were appointed a Provisional Board of Directors to establish a new public copartnership or company in Calcutta with a capital of 20 lakhs of rupees, or £200,000, to be called 'The India General Steam Navigation Company' for the purpose of providing and navigating steam vessels on the Ganges, the Hooghli, the Jumna, and the other great rivers of India and their branches and tributaries, and to be afterwards extended with increased capital when circumstances may render it advisable, and thereby to carry on the trade and business of carriers of passengers, and of merchandise and other cargo for hire.'

The first route of the new company was to be the classic run from Calcutta to Allahabad, but there were many difficulties before a paying service was established. The first steamer built for the company, the *Sir Herbert Maddock*, was lost in the Ganges on her second voyage. Rival companies were formed, though none survived for very long, and there were calls on the shareholders for more capital and quarrels among the directors.

The provision of coal supplies was a great problem. There were, of course, no railways, and it would not have been profitable to carry coal in the steamers, so it was moved to the riverside depots in river sailing boats. This was twenty years before the economical compound marine engine revolutionised water transport, and the old fashioned simple engines of the steamers ate vast quantities of coal. There had to be dumps all the way up the Ganges to enable them to refuel regularly. By the time the coal had reached some of those dumps (and it took months to get there from Calcutta) it cost so much that the coal bills in some of those early years were nearly 40 per cent of the total working expenses of the company.

The India General played its part in the re-establishment of law and order in India after the troubles of 1857, usually called in Britain the Indian Mutiny. All their ships were chartered for troop carrying at rates very profitable to the company. In 1857 the company paid a thirty per cent dividend, and in 1858 the profits of the one year exceeded the total capital and yielded a dividend of seventy-two per cent. Even then a lot of money was wisely ploughed back into new ships and shore facilities, so that by 1859 the India General had ten steamers and ten barges. At the same time a revolutionary step was taken when Captain Wheeler of the steamer *Madras*, instead of towing one big barge behind his steamer experimented with towing two, one lashed at either side. He was reprimanded for his rashness, but from then on steamers always towed in this way and they still do when in the rivers. Such a tow is much easier to handle, safer and more economical in smooth, narrow, waters than one comprising barges trailing on hundreds of feet of rope astern.

But, after the Mutiny, despite these innovations, there were years of difficulty. Prosperity brought more rivals on to the big rivers. The most dangerous of these proved to be the Rivers Steam Navigation Company, founded by one of the India General's own captains, J. H. Williamson of the *General MacLeod* and the *Madras* (the *Madras* seems to have bred enterprising skippers). For years these two companies followed parallel and often highly competitive courses, until in 1889 they began, by agreement, to work together as 'The Joint Steamer Companies'.

The railways took more and more of the Ganges trade as the 1860s advanced. The main railway line ran on the south bank of the river and the steamer companies therefore tried to concentrate on the trade to the towns of the north bank. Not surprisingly perhaps, this unbalanced trade did not prove very profitable, and in 1864 the policy had to be abandoned. It was then that the India General and the Rivers Steam began to look eastwards, away from the Ganges Valley to the waters of the great Brahmaputra, to the big rivers of the country which was to become East Pakistan and of Assam. And it was there that their real destiny lay.

In the early 1860s the efforts of the adventurers who had first attempted to transplant tea bushes from China to Assam (and then found local wild tea growing alongside their plantations) began to earn their reward. Until then Assam had been a most forsaken province of British India. The only means of communications with the outside world was by a government owned steamer which left Calcutta once every six weeks. But the Assam line, soon to become one of the great inland water services of the world, began when the India General came to an arrangement with the government under which they took over this service for six months.

Unlike the Ganges, which flows through densely populated districts, the great Brahmaputra passes through what in the early 1860s was a practically unknown country, sparsely inhabited and with practically nothing of worth to export. The whole gamble depended upon one thing—tea. Tea was a very expensive item in Europe in those days, it came mostly from China in the fully rigged sailing ships of which the *Cutty Sark*, now preserved in drydock at Greenwich, was always among the most famous. Wild tea was found in Assam in 1823, and it had been shipped to Europe since 1837, but even in 1860 tea growing was still a small industry. It was soon due to develop very quickly. The Suez Canal, the compound engined steamship, and the river steamer service made this possible between them. And, with the tea industry, Assam itself developed. As one of its administrators said more than fifty years ago, 'The history of Assam is the history of tea.'

Year by year the trade up the Ganges declined. By 1864 the railway had reached Allahabad. In the same years the great irrigation systems of the Punjab and northern India were begun. They were to revolutionise life in these parts of Asia, but they took vast quantities of water during the dry season which left the river below the proper navigable level. Besides this, the absence of water meant that the river began to silt up and the channels became blocked to the larger steamers. On one occasion a steamer took five months to get to Allahabad and back. At each shoal the cargo was taken out and placed in river sailing boats while the steamer was worked over the shallow water.

But in 1864 the Assam tea industry began to boom. There was a rush of investment and many new tea gardens were established. Sparsely populated as it was Assam could not provide the workers for these new gardens and they had to be recruited and brought in from other parts of India. When they and their families were duly installed, all the food they ate had at first to be imported into Assam too. Tea labourers were recruited by the thousand in

Madras, Bihar, the Central Provinces, and the Ganges Valley, and they all poured up the river into Assam. The steamers were fitted with upper decks to accommodate more passengers (and they kept those upper decks ever afterwards) and even the great barges were fitted out for passenger carrying too. The share capital of the steamer companies was rapidly increased and more and more ships were bought. Existing steamers were lengthened so that they could carry more new workers up river and move tea down. By 1874, only ten years after the railway reached Allahabad and the Assam boom had started, the India General closed down the Ganges route altogether and began to concentrate entirely on Assam.

The company's pilots had begun to feel their way through the labyrinth of the Sunderbans with a view to setting up a route through what is now East Pakistan to the Brahmaputra as an alternative to the Hooghli—Ganges route previously in use. By 1871 this route was established, though it was to prove a dangerous channel in which many steamers and barges have been lost over the years. On the up-river journey Pakistan is entered in the Sunderbans jungle. Then the steamers and their great barges swing north to Khulna, and from there east to Barisal. From here they go up the great Brahmaputra, past the junction with the Ganges at Goalundo, and up the wide, ever changing river to the Assam border, and on up the long narrow valley. Small steamers can go to the borders of the almost unknown beyond Dibrugarh.

This great trade route showed the steamer companies the possibilities of the eastern parts of the alluvial plain, which are now East Pakistan. Within twenty-five years an enormous trade had developed in carrying jute from Dacca, Narayanganj and Chandpur to Calcutta for export and this became the largest part in bulk, though not in value, of the company's business. At the same time, in the early 1870s, the compound engine was introduced in the river steamers, with the spectacular result that fuel consumption was almost immediately halved.

Until the 1880s every steamer and every barge had had a British captain, some of them with deep sea master's certificates.

Some steamers carried two certificated British mates, some barges had the British master's wife and family on board. To employ such people was costly and unnecessary when Noakhali, Tipperah and Chittagong were the homes of some of the finest watermen in the world. So the steamer companies began to train men from these districts to command first barges and then steamers. The first barge to have an Indian commander was the *Mutlah* in 1883. The first Indian to command a big steamer towing barges was a Muslim, Hanif the Serang, who took over the *Sultan*, built in 1877. A cadre of skilled qualified masters, mates, and later engineers, rapidly grew up in Noakhali and Chittagong and by 1910 there were only nine European commanders left. The last one ceased to serve afloat in the 1920s. By then the network of the companies' services looked very much as it was to look twenty-five years later, when India and Pakistan became independent.

Some of the side paddle steamers in use on the Brahmaputra today are, like the river sailing boats, modern relics of an earlier age of commerce. Coal burning, hand fired—orders transmitted from bridge to engine room by jangling gongs—there is nothing like them left in Britain except the National Maritime Museum's splendid *Old Trafford*. And as far as I know, there is only one vessel, the passenger steamer *Ticonderoga*, preserved at the Shelburne Museum, in North America. The much admired *Ti*, with her simple engine and 'walking beam' transmission of power from piston to paddle wheels is unique. But until recently there were steamers on the big rivers which were older than she is, and differed only in having compound engines, with the attendant direct operation of piston rod and crankshaft; and in being less gaily painted and less comfortably fitted out.

To see them was to move back into the great age of American steamboating, when the continent was opening up to the chunk of feathering paddles and the musical hoots of the whistles. A big steamer is an impressive sight, tearing along between the high walls of jungle in a narrow river, a smother of foam at her bow and her decks filled with passengers. She comprises two distinct parts, a long shallow hull with boilers and engines, or diesels, amidships, and a light superstructure covering her whole length with an upper deck and with a roof against the monsoon rains, through which the funnel projects (page 69). Her navigation bridge is on top of this roof and the bridge and roof are reinforced with a criss-cross of steel cables against the awful power of the north-westers which have been known to tear a steamer apart and roll her over to destruction.

The steamer progresses with no sound except the 'whoosh, whoosh' of the paddles in the water. This noise, which sounds from the river bank like 'chunk, chunk', goes on all day and every day on all the main rivers of East Pakistan. At night the steamers go on, finding their way by the lifetime's experience of their masters and by the glare of an enormous searchlight. It is a strange feeling to stand on the foredeck of a steamer and watch the banks, yellow in the carbon arc light, flash by as the beam, filled with a million insects, dodges this way and that while the officer of the watch swivels the remote control wheel, ceaselessly peering through the night. The warm, damp air blows steadily. All is silent except for the paddles and the rush of the water. On the decks behind the blanketed forms of hundreds of passengers lie asleep. They sleep soundly, in faith in God, and because they have known the steamers all their lives, as their fathers, and their grandfathers, and their great grandfathers did before them.

Part 2

BEHIND THE DESERT SHORE

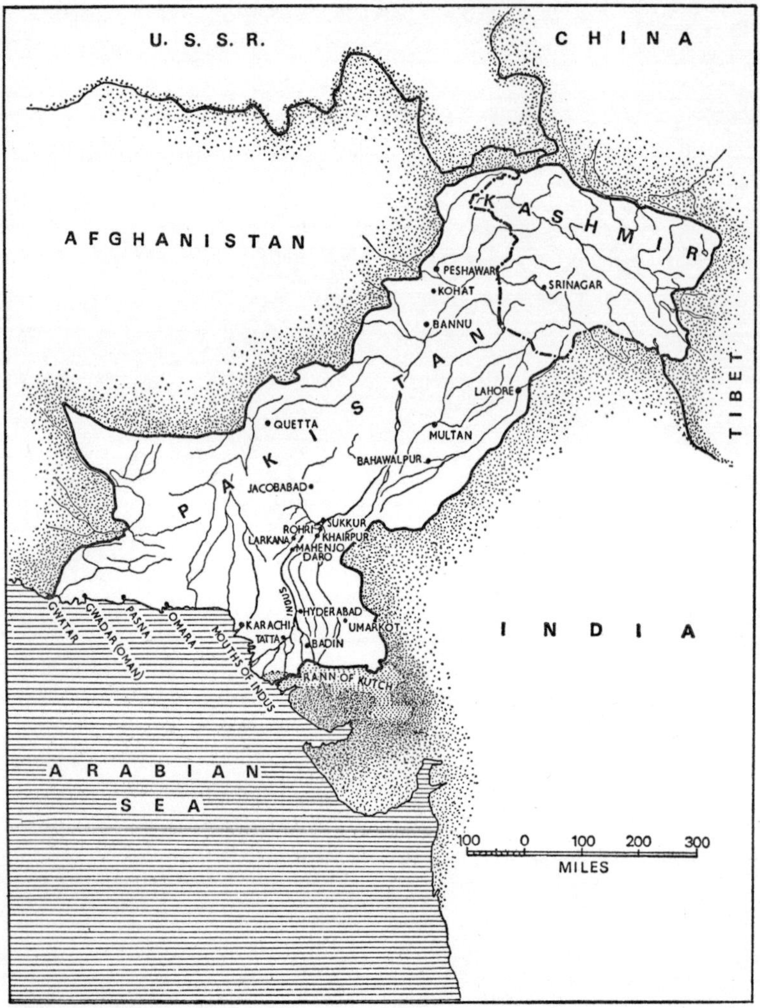

West Pakistan

Seven

THE KARACHI FISHERMEN

More than a thousand miles away from Dacca across India is the chief port and former capital city of Pakistan, Karachi, standing between the Arabian Sea and the great desert of Sind, a white new city in a yellow land. To the north and west of Karachi stretches the great area of West Pakistan, nearly six times as large as the eastern province, but with only three-quarters of its population. West Pakistan stretches almost from the Soviet Union to the Gulf of Oman, from the desert coast to the High Pamir, from Persia to the India plains (Map 2).

It, too, depends for its life on rivers. But in this Province the dependence is of a different kind. Here the land is high and, for the most part very dry. The rivers flow down from the Hindu Kush and the High Pamir and the Himalayas through fertile valleys set like green gems among the jagged wastes of rock. They break through gorges down into the great plains of West Pakistan and across these plains they flow for hundreds of miles to the sea.

On each side of the main rivers there stretches network after network of irrigation canals and on these canals the population, which has expanded enormously in the century since the rivers were seriously tapped for large scale irrigation, is absolutely dependent. As you enter a canal zone from the surrounding semi-desert at the sharp line where the cultivation begins everything changes. The air, instead of being dry and thin, is at once damp and cool, smelling of fertility and life. Bright coloured birds fly in and out of the deep shade of the thick trees. Parrots scream, cattle are at the water's edge, crops and signs of people, villages, roads, boats are everywhere.

In spite of irrigation the Western Province of Pakistan is still very sparsely peopled in comparison with the East. The rivers run parallel with roads and railways for much of their vast length. When they ran through largely empty country there was little commerce and few people to be carried on them. Today so much of their water is taken to feed mankind that only a small fraction of what once poured out into the Indian Ocean now reaches the sea, and the rivers are much reduced potential highways.

Nevertheless, from the rafts made of frameworks of wooden poles lashed to inflated bullock skins from which the fishermen of Swat trail their lines in the shallow rapids to the 60ft long outrigger canoes of the Karachi fishermen, there are boats on the big rivers of West Pakistan and the estuary of the Indus, through which all the rivers find their way to the sea. Sukkur, 300 miles up the Indus from the Arabian Sea, is a river port for great flat-bottomed, square-sided scows which come sailing downstream. They are rowed back for hundreds of miles with sweeps 30ft long pulled by rows of sweating oarsmen pacing backwards and forwards on their decks. In the main rivers and the labyrinths of canals, and the marshes of Sind near the sea, the local watermen use a type of decked punt which may be among the oldest sophisticated boats in the world. On the Kabul river and the Upper Indus, flat-bottomed shallow boats with pointed ends carry wood and hay, stone and sugar cane; and there is a small, surprising, thriving boatbuilding industry in the lovely Peshawar valley, where the Khyber Pass breaks down from Afghanistan into the plains.

We travelled by freighter round India from East Pakistan to the Western Province, from Chittagong to Karachi, calling in at Colombo on the way. Lying in the river Karnafuli at Chittagong was a brigantine with an auxiliary engine which had come up from Burma. She looked very big amongst the *balams* and *sampans* at anchor around her. It was April and the north-westers might have started at any time, but there were still river boats along the sandy shore of the bay to the north of us as we left the estuary for the open sea.

Page 141 (*above*) Fishermen making up nets on the wharf by Karachi's fishing boat harbour; (*below*) the almost finished planking of a *hora* of the largest kind still shows gaps at the turn of the bilge. It is a flimsy shell awaiting the strengthening inserted frames

Page 142 (*above*) A small cargo or ferry boat in the Peshawar Valley. She has the conventionalised flower pattern on the bows. Astern of her is a large cargo boat of the Kabul River; (*below*) a bullock skin ferry raft, ferry wharf and ferry boy on the Swat River

The passage was uneventful, apart from one suicide. The master of our steamer told us there were one or two among the crowded deck passengers on every voyage. The steamer of about 8,000 tons had been making the voyage round to Karachi and back again to Chittagong for several years already and she almost knew the way by herself. There were the usual sights of the Indian Ocean, flying fish and porpoises playing around the bows and in our wake, the east coast of Ceylon silhouetted at sunset, the palm-fringed west coast south of Colombo, the outrigger dugout canoes fishing far off shore. While we were lying in Colombo the *Glory of the Sea,* a brigantine from the Maldives with the single topsails and a long jib-boom, a ship of 150 years ago, sailed in between the breakwaters and beat up the harbour, passing under our stern, to an anchorage right inside. This lovely ship had become, perhaps, the last square rigged sailing ship to earn her living by carrying cargo at sea which the world will ever know.

A few days later we were lying off Karachi, heaving to the gentle swell and waiting for the tide to let us up to our berth. That morning, while we were still out of sight of the low coast, we had met our first *hora.* She was not more than 30ft long and perhaps 5ft wide, a sailing canoe with an outrigger which could be used either as weight or float, and a balance board out over the water on the other side. Ten miles off shore a boy stood unconcerned on the middle of the balance board, holding the rope which stretched from its end to the mast head. As she rolled to the swell and to the regular lessening and strengthening of the pressure of the wind on her great lateen sail as she moved up and down and in and out of the lee of the waves, his feet were either abruptly almost dipping in the Arabian Sea or far above it. She was sailing quickly further away from the land, and she would probably be out fishing for twenty-four hours or more. She was an open boat with no shelter, no cooking space except for a fire on the short foredeck, no place for the crew to relieve themselves, hardly anywhere to lie down. But the sun was warm, the weather predictable or anyway very unlikely to change, and this was the way the boy made his living and helped to feed the family of brothers and sisters playing on the beach of Ibrahim Hyderi, the fishing village on the shore of the most northerly of the creeks at the mouth of the Indus, east and south of Karachi.

The desert shore of the Arabian Sea where it washes the coast of West Pakistan is in two quite different parts. The first, stretching from the Persian frontier to just east of Karachi, comprises sandy beaches backed by low crumbling cliffs. At some seasons of the year these beaches are alive with crabs which sidle away as one walks through them. At other times turtles drag themselves up out of the sea to bury their eggs in the hot sand. Behind the cliffs is a desolate hinterland, hundreds of miles of glaring rock and sand, sprinkled with grey cactus. Big lizards scuttle away as you drive along the tracks, and such settlements as there are are poor and primitive. Parts of this desert are pregnant with latent life and turn briefly green after the rare seasonal showers of rain.

East of Karachi the coast turns abruptly through 90° to run north and south and at the same time it changes equally suddenly in nature. It becomes a maze of creeks and saltings, tidal rivers and low muddy islands covered with mangrove bushes. This water wilderness comprises the mouth of the River Indus, much reduced in its lower reaches by the demands of the irrigation schemes further up its course, but still a great river, here ending its journey of nearly 2,000 miles from the heart of the Himalayas to the Arabian Sea. So extensive is the system of sheltered waterways which make up its delta that it is possible, the boatmen say, for a local craft to work with a cargo from a point near Karachi right down through the Indus delta into the maze of saltings of the Rann of Kutch and on into Indian waters, without ever going out into the open sea.

Karachi lies on the northern edge of this labyrinth of mud and mangrove, sand and swamp, separated from it by a belt of desert a few miles wide. Karachi harbour was perhaps once one of the streams of the Indus delta, but, if so, that was a very long time ago. Almost within living memory it was a shallow sandy inlet, filled with mangrove swamps, with a small settlement of poor fishermen at one end of it. It was a little known and less used creek on the edge of the desert. But the spread northwards of British administration; irrigation and the consequent increase in the population of the hinterland; and finally the coming of the railway down the Indus valley to the coast from Lahore in the far north of the Punjab, meant that there was use for a port at the mouth of the Indus, and money to be made there. Karachi, between the delta and the desert, was the natural site. So the bar across the entrance to the creek was dredged away, and the channel inside cut out deeper and deeper as the years went by. Quays and wharves were built, and shipyards, and marshalling yards and dry-docks. And all the time the settlement around grew and grew from a village to a town and a town to a great city.

When the Indian sub-continent was partitioned and Pakistan created in two parts, Karachi became its first capital, and the population, the city, and the port grew almost explosively. With them grew the local market for fish, the demand for firewood (mangrove wood brought up by boat from the swamps of the Indus delta) and for boats for general watermen's duties about the harbour. Soon the fishing industry at the fishing boat harbour inside the main harbour of Karachi, and at Ibrahim Hyderi, 5-6 miles away across the desert on Korangi, the northermost creek of the delta, was on a far larger scale than it ever had been in the days when most of the population was dependent on fishing for its life.

The traditional boats of this coast were the result of the introduction of Arab and European ideas about boatbuilding along the coasts of India and Africa and in the Persian Gulf. Boats like the Arab *bhums* and *baggalas* and the Indian *kotias* (page 106) came into Karachi from the north and the south, and the local boatbuilders, some of whom were men who had moved up from the south, copied them in miniature and produced types which soon became locally traditional. Of these the principal were the *bheddi* and the *bhart*.

The *bheddi* (page 123, Figs 19, 20 & 21) is a short keeled boat with long overhanging bow, of the type the Arabs call *grab*, and a sloping transom stern. Her keel is parallel with the water line. Her quarters are very full with flat buttocks and her greatest

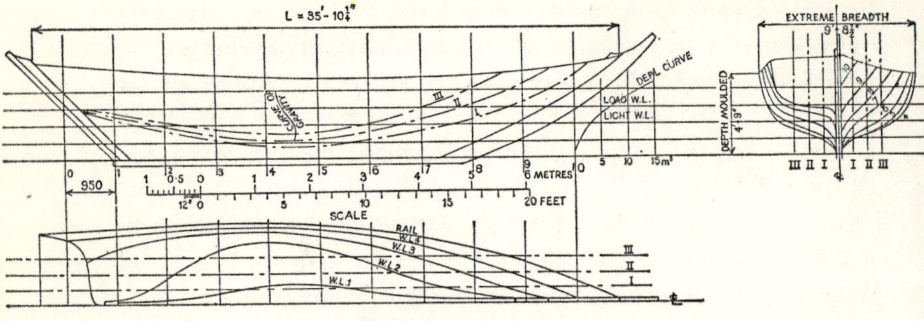

19 Lines of a small *bheddi*

beam is well aft—this latter characteristic is one of her most conspicuous features. She has a marked rise of floor, hollow garboards and a hard turn of bilge. The water lines are often quite hollow at the bow and in the run. She has long fixed decks fore and aft, though the greater part of her is open. Most *bheddis* have inside ballast of rocks and the larger ones have sandbags on deck as well. The smallest ones have balance boards.

Most *bheddis* are big boats, 40-70ft long. They are rigged with great, Arab-style settee sails, a large mainsail and a small mizzen for the light winter breezes. A smaller mainsail is used only in the stronger winds of summer when the mizzen mast is sometimes unstepped. Depending on her size and the season of the year, a *bheddi* can set anything from about 350 to 1,500sq ft of cotton sails. The *bheddi* is a beautiful and seaworthy type of boat, easily driven. As the American nautical historian, Howard I. Chapelle has said, she is 'a boat one would like to have'.

She is more than that. It has for many years been a matter of general agreement amongst those who know them that West Pakistan fishing boats are good looking and well built and that they are manned by enterprising fishermen who go far out to sea and land good catches. Some years ago the Pakistan Government asked the Food and Agriculture Organisation of the United Nations to advise on how the boats might be improved and

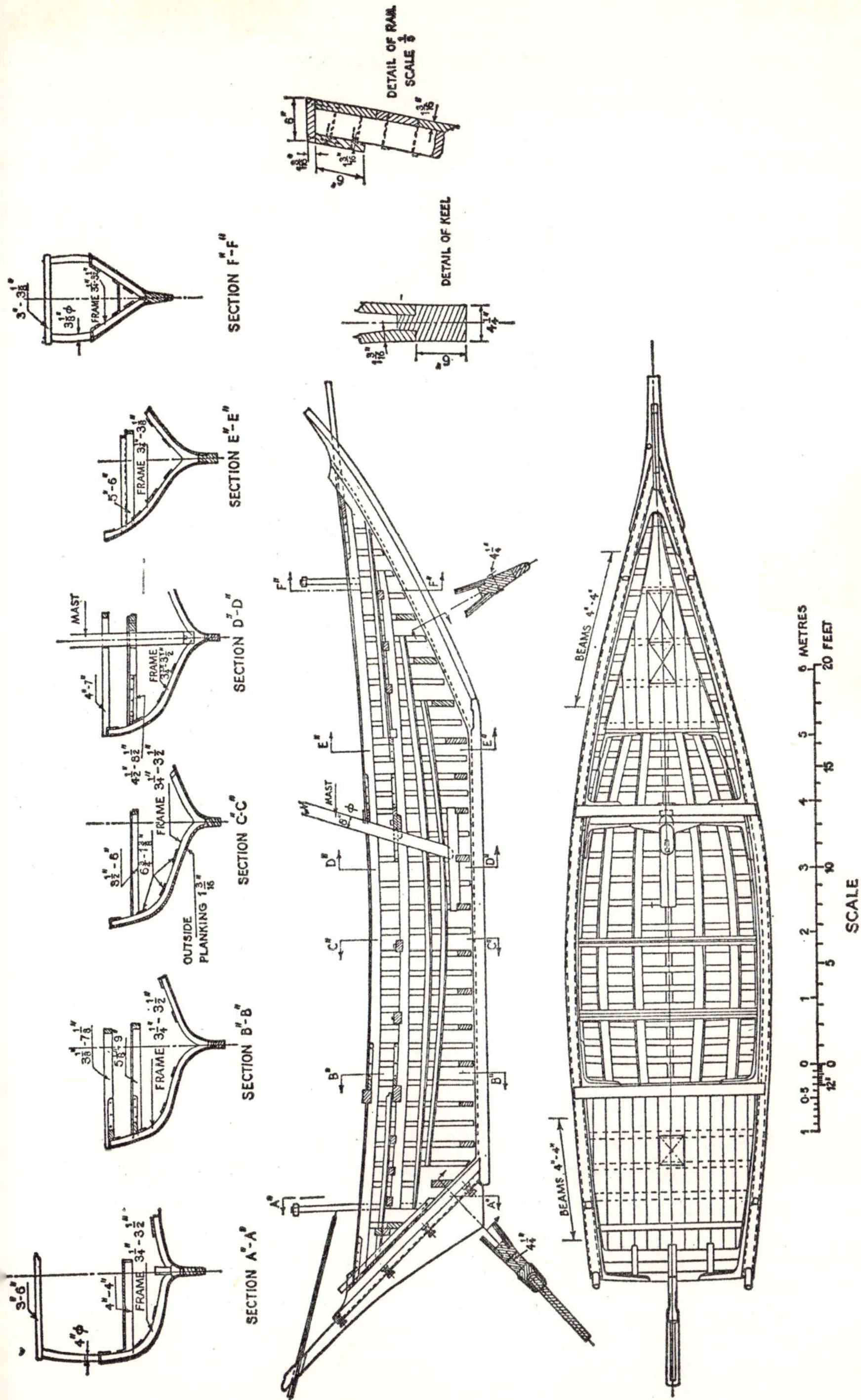

20 Construction drawing of a medium sized *bheddi*

21 Sail and sheer plan of a medium sized *bheddi*

whether European or American types of fishing boats might not be more efficient for the work they have to do. The FAO carried out a detailed examination of the boats, the first such detailed examination which had ever been made of a family of what it was at one time the fashion among nautical archaeologists to call 'primitive craft'. The results should end the use of this term once and for all. Model tests in the Swedish State Shipbuilding Experimental Tank, in which results from models of European fishing boats were compared with results from tests of models of the Pakistan boats, proved the Pakistan boats to be of very high quality, and the *bheddi* to be the best. The FAO teams found it possible to say in their report that, 'It is reasonable to state that the Pakistani boats are equally good, if not better, regarding resistance characteristics, than typical fishing boats in Europe today'. The FAO's naval architects designed an ideal fishing craft for the Karachi fishery, a lateen rigged boat with a kerosene auxiliary engine, which is in fact a big *bheddi*, slightly more powerful in her sections, with a more marked sheer, a much improved stern, and of heavier construction than that traditional in Pakistan. As the report of the naval architects said, ' . . . the present Pakistani boats are of very good design and it is rather difficult to propose any type of hull which is more efficient. Therefore, in building new boats, one should keep to the present type for purely technical reasons, in addition to the psychological fact that fishermen are always more willing to use mechanised boats of a familiar type, than to try new types which look and might behave quite differently from those they have been using'.

A *bheddi* has a box on deck for fresh fish and ice and a small hold space or 'room', as it would have been called in most British open sailing fishing boats, for nets, cooking utensils, the fresh-water tank or breakers, and salt for curing. Water is heated, and the crew's very simple food is cooked, on an open fire in a brick hearth. The fishing methods used all involve nets, mostly gill nets, nowadays made from nylon cord bought cheaply in bulk. Wooden floats keep the head of the net on the surface and lead sinkers hold the bottom down. A big *bheddi* will carry 1,500ft of nets, 18-40ft deep.

She will also carry as many as twelve men. For the master the Arab term *nakhoda* is used. 50 per cent of the value of the catch goes to the owners of the boat, 50 per cent to the crew, and the *nakhoda* gets twice the seamen's share. If he owns the boat the *nakhoda* gets the owner's share but then customarily forfeits his master's portion.

A *bheddi* may travel 150 miles up the coast towards the Persian Gulf in search of fish. If she is lucky she may bring back 500-600 big fish after a five day trip. They are preserved in the great wooden box, packed with smashed ice, on the open deck. Sometimes *bheddis* go out for longer, but ice will not last more than four or five days in the Arabian Sea, even in winter, and on the longer trips the fish are preserved by beginning a salt curing process on board.

Although building costs are markedly lower than those of Europe and North America, a big *bheddi* with her equipment still represents a considerable investment for a Pakistani peasant fisherman. In the early nineteen fifties it cost from about £400 to £1,500 to build a *bheddi*, according to size, and another £1,500 or more to fit her out with nets. There is no wood behind the desert shore and almost all the materials of which she was built had to be imported. The teak for the keel, stern and sternpost and planking, came from Burma, India and Malaya. The wood for the frames (acacia for the straight runs) came from India, as did the masts, which cost perhaps £65 each, and the yards for the big summer lateen sails. The small winter sails were set from bamboo yards from up the Indus and from East Pakistan. The sails themselves were made of cotton fabrics manufactured in Pakistan, the big foresails from handwoven cloth, the little mizzens from machine woven drill. The rigging was locally made on the beach as were the blocks, anchors and cables. The paint for decoration of bow and stern was locally made and the greater part of the hull was treated with a crude fish oil preparation, which made the boats look very smart and shiny when new, but also made them smell.

For all her virtues there is evidence that the classical sailing *bheddi* was already a dying type in the 1950s. Laid up *bheddis* could be seen on the beaches around Karachi most of the year round. I never found a *bheddi* under construction and the fishermen themselves tended to speak of the *bheddi* as a type of craft slowly being replaced by the larger size of an entirely different kind of sailing boat, the *hora*.

As a result of the absence of *bheddis* being built on the beaches around Karachi I was never able to satisfy myself completely on one fundamental question about their construction. But nevertheless there is very little doubt as to the answer. The question is whether they are built on pre-erected frames like European skeleton built craft, or whether the planks are edge joined and the frames inserted after the main part of the shell of planking has been erected, like the boats of East Pakistan. All the evidence pointed to the latter. The fishermen with whom I talked said the *bheddis* were built by making the shell of planks first of all and then inserting framing to fit and hold the boat in shape. The framing of some old *bheddis*, although they were not in a state of disintegration sufficient for one to be able to confirm that the planks were joined together edge to edge, had certainly not been erected as a skeleton before the planks were nailed to it. Indeed, it comprised odds and ends of grown timber bands of irregular shape and there had been no attempt to join up the various pieces, so that the planking itself provided the only continuity in the boat's construction. I do not think these craft could possibly have held together on the sunbaked beaches, much less in the seas of the monsoon, if the planks had not been joined together. But the strongest evidence rests in the methods used in building that other type of local fishing boat, the *hora* (See page 154).

The smallest *bheddis* are the Karachi 'bunder boats', the watermen's boats of the busy harbour. Besides their rock ballast, these use balance boards to keep upright. The bunder boat, with her gay awning aft and the plastic covered seat cushions on the benches under it, is the great recreational boat of the neighbourhood. Beamy, roomy, and reasonably stable, she is nevertheless lively enough, with her huge sail, to be fun when a breeze comes.

The *bhart* is a *bheddi* with a pointed sloping stern instead of the broad transom. She bears the same relation to the *bheddi* as the pointed sterned Arab *bhum* does to the *baggala*. Because in the same length, with the maximum beam still well aft, the lines at the stern must be brought to a point, she seems more beamy and fuller in section than her sister, though in fact the lines are very similar. I saw a few *bharts* fitted out for fishing, but the *bhart* is really the big cargo carrier of the northern Indus delta and lines of them were to be seen in the cold weather discharging their loads, principally mangrove wood for the cooking fires of Karachi, into camel carts at the tideline on the beaches of Ibrahim Hyderi (page 123).

The *bhart* has a burdensome hull to drive and in some craft

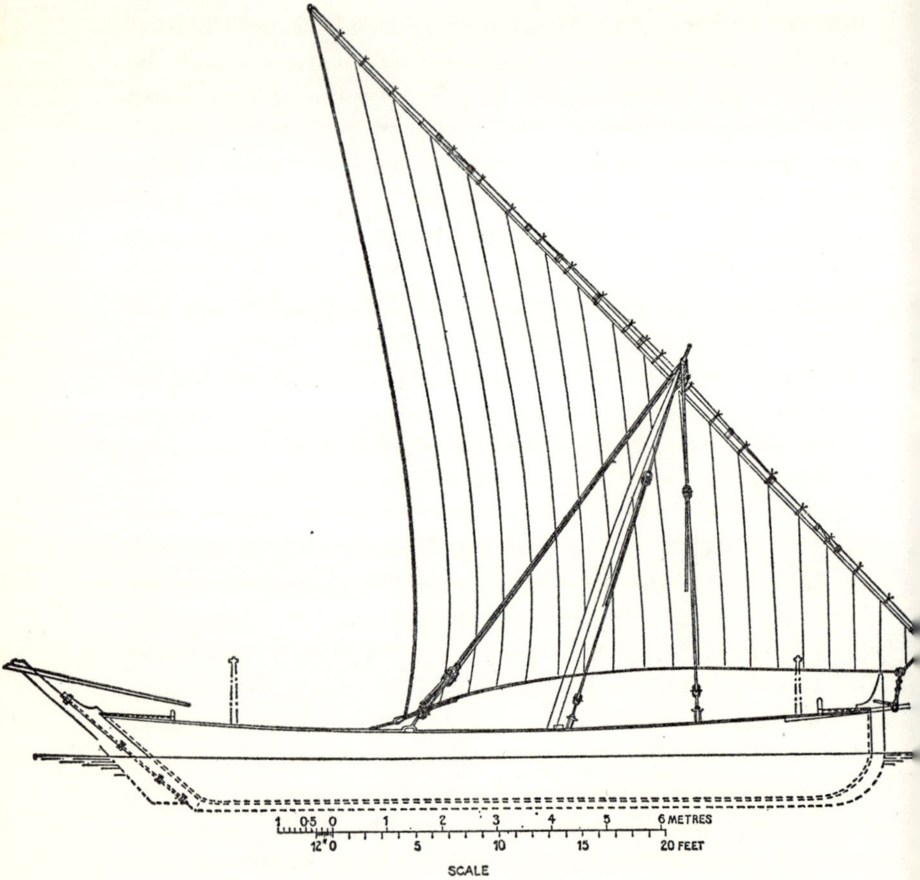

22 Sail and sheer plan of a medium sized *hora*

the mizzen mast appears to be stepped permanently. When piled high with deck cargo she is sometimes fitted with movable side-boards above her bulwarks. *Bharts* are often very well maintained, as are many of the Karachi craft, with sheer line picked out in a colour pattern, and decorated stern head and sternpost. She sometimes has vestigial oculi on her quarters. The rudder head is often carried far above the sternpost, so that the tiller, decorated with bands of white paint, points downwards to the deck at an angle of 30-40°.

The *bhart* and the *bheddi* are splendid, handsome craft, but they are expensive and complicated to build, they need a lot of timber and their sharp lines and steep rise of hull mean that they have difficult curves to plank and frame, and that they cannot lie upright on the beach at low tide but have to be held up with legs (page 123) like the Bristol Channel pilot cutters used to when they took the ground in one of the drying harbours of south-western Britain. Moreover they are deep and if this makes them sail well it also means that they have to be unloaded of their fish at a wharf, either when they are afloat or when they are lying propped up alongside it, or by means of another, smaller, shallower boat which can carry their catch ashore while they lie off a beach in deeper water.

All these factors, but most of all that of expense, seem to have lead to the development of a cheaper, altogether simpler, if less handsome, seaworthy, and attractive, type of fishing boat at Karachi. These are the *horas* (page 124 and Fig 22) and there are three main types of them, the *toni*, the *ekdar hora* and the *hora* proper, or so their owners and crews told us when we talked with them on the beaches of Ibrahim Hyderi and sailed with them for long hot days off the desert shore.

The *horas* are almost all fishing boats, though a few carry cargoes in the Indus creeks and, especially during the monsoon when the seas can be too rough even for a Karachi fisherman, some do general watermen's work in the harbour. The most conspicuous and notable thing about *horas* is that the three types taken together appear to present a complete evolutionary series from the dugout to the large, fully framed and planked up sea-going fishing boat. And, as with the clinker built boats of the Khasi Hills and the plains of Sylhet, *horas* at all the different stages in the evolutionary tree go on existing side by side today, each fulfilling the original function it fulfilled when it was first evolved. The *horas* begin, if you like to put it that way, at the *toni* with a dugout, and, in ascending order of size, go on through the dugout with added planks and the plank built boat with the dugout base, to end in fully plank built boats up to 68ft or more in length.

As far as I could determine, all the plank built, or partly plank built, *horas* are built by the same method. They are first planked up, the strakes being joined edge to edge, not with the complicated *patam loha* fastening of East Pakistan, but with single metal pins. The frames are subsequently cut to fit the planking and inserted into it. There is a strong family likeness running through all the *horas.* Apart from the fact that they are all built the same way, a steeply raking sternpost with a long, narrow, rudder lashed to it which does not project below the long straight keel; a rounded forefoot and straight stem; head ornaments and a low freeboard, are characteristic of these long narrow boats of all sizes.

The name seems to be another version of *huri* or *hori*, the term used by some Arabs to describe a simple plank-extended dugout canoe, usually of Indian origin. In Ceylon a plank-extended dugout with an outrigger is called an *oru.*

But in the largest, fully plank built, *horas* it is evident that influences other than the dugout have been at work. The section shapes change markedly once a certain size is reached. The deep U of the dugout gives way to rather flat floors and sometimes a rather sudden turn of bilge and flaring sides. The length-beam ratio changes from 1 in 7 or 8 of the smaller *horas* to 1 in 4 or 5, though in the middle sizes two *horas* of the same overall length may lie side by side on the beach, one long and excessively narrow and the other quite a beamy craft. It might be conjectured that the larger *horas* have developed because people used to working with plank-extended dugouts found themselves prospering and needed larger, but cheap boats which were built for them by men used to building *bheddis* and *bharts* and other traditional Arab and Indian sailing craft.

The little *toni* is an ordinary Indian dugout made in Calicut, of the kind which is to be found in varying forms all the way from Southern India, up the West Coast, around the Persian Gulf and down the coast of Africa. The Karachi type is one of the simpler variants. She is 6-20ft long, flat sheered, with little ornament save paint, the solid wood which comprise bow and stern pierced for two ropes. She is not expanded, but on the contrary, her sides often curve inwards into a 'tumble home'. She has inside transverse bands, left when she was hollowed out, in low relief at intervals across the bottom and up the sides. These are purely ornamental and presumably represent in their present form an attempt on the part of the makers to imitate a conspicuous feature of the lighter, more efficient, more expensive, and therefore more prestigious, plank built boat. The modern *toni* frequently has substantial rough, sawn frames and half frames as well as these vestiges, but they are usually added by the owner as the canoe grows older and weaker.

Tonis are paddled or rowed by one or two men. Even the smallest of them are sometimes equipped with a short mast and a small lateen sail set from a very light yard. This sail is used off the wind even under what appear to be very dangerous conditions. But the *toni*, although used to communicate between the islands in Karachi harbour and the shore—even during the monsoon—is rarely, if ever, seen in the open sea. *Tonis* are used as tenders to larger fishing craft, and the larger *horas* and *bheddis* often carry one on the quarter. When used as fishing boats inside the harbour cast nets and hand lines are likely to be their owners' fishing gear.

The term *ekdar hora* means, literally, a *hora* built out of one piece of wood, but in practice it means a large fishing canoe built of planks on a dugout base. The term appears to be used fairly loosely by the fishermen themselves to describe a whole group of boats ranging from a dugout with a few planks added to its sides to a great, fully planked up boat which may be as much as 45ft long. Strictly speaking, the term should be confined to boats which have a dugout in their construction somewhere, but it is used here as a type name for all those *horas* which follow the dugout in their general proportions.

The dugout based *ekdar hora* shows a fine combination of reality and symbol, for her sawn frames are rarely placed to coincide with the raised bands which remain visible on the bottom and sides of the basic dugout. In the smaller boats the dugout determines the overall length of the vessel, since she narrows away at bow and stern as the dugout dictates. Even with these little boats the planks may extend the sides so that the dugout base is less than half the depth of the finished boat, while the characteristic steeply sloping sternpost and vertical stern of the *hora* are built on.

With the next larger size of *ekdar hora* it is difficult to see where the dugout ends and the planks begin. The basic dugout her ends sawn off, is extended with plank construction at bow and stern, as well as above her sides, so that the finished boat is sometimes twice as long as the original dugout. When, in an old *hora* of this type, the dugout itself has been repaired with planking let into its 'skin', it becomes quite a problem to tell whether she is based on a dugout or whether she is a boat built wholly of planks.

In recent years the importing of dugouts from Calicut in India into Pakistan has at times been difficult. So some even of the smallest *horas* are now built wholly of planks. The majority of them are still close imitations in dimensions and proportions of the plank-extended dugouts. But the adoption of planks has freed the *hora* from the limitations of the dugout's basic form, and I saw tiny *horas*, only 15ft long, under construction which had the flatter sections and broader beam which show the influence of the *bheddi* and other basically Arab type of small sailing ship.

The *ekdar hora*, with her canoe-like proportions, is a fast, unstable, sailing boat. She cannot sail at all, whatever her size, without some kind of balancing device. Depending on her size, the season of the year, and the sort of waters in which she is fishing, this can be anything from a single shifting balance board—which is changed from side to side, tack to tack, and on which a member of the *hora*'s crew will sit or stand, agilely scuttling backwards and forwards with catlike movements up and down the board as the varying wind may require him to exert greater or less moment to keep the hull upright in the water—to a lash up of two fixed balance boards on one side and an outrigger float on two long poles on the other (page 124).

An *ekdar hora* working habitually in the creeks of Karachi harbour may, during the calm cool weather of the winter months, have no more aids to stability than one balance board. A boat of identical size and shape, working in more exposed waters during the monsoon, may have double balance boards and an outrigger. Under different conditions she may have the outrigger alone or with a single fixed balance board. Her own particular shape and the sailing qualities imposed by this will also determine the balancing devices she needs to use.

The outrigger float, sometimes cut from solid timber but perhaps more often built up from laminations, has a sharp entrance flaring out rapidly to a very flat section in the middle, so that it appears to derive its lift not only from its own buoyancy but also from a planing effect, and it slows up the boat less than might be expected. The outrigger poles are braced with cross pieces and sometimes with stays from their outer ends to bow and stern. When there are two fixed balance boards that nearest the bow is longer than the other and is braced with a heavy rope, often fitted with a tackle, from the mast head.

A big canoe-like *ekdar hora*, expertly handled and with a crew of four or five men, sails extremely well off the wind and on a reach, and can make up to windward well enough on one tack, the tack on which the wind is blowing on the side opposite to her fixed outrigger float. In the light airs of winter she will sail often with the wind on the same side as the outrigger, which will sometimes lift out of the water. Sailing in and out of Karachi harbour, or one of the creeks of the Indus, she must on occasion do the same in the strong winds and rough seas of the monsoon. Then great agility on the balance board is called for, to keep the float near the surface of the water, not above it and not swinging underneath so that the boat is slowed, or so slewed round as to become uncontrollable.

Balance boardmanship is an art all of its own and in its finer forms represents one of the world's most skilled manifestations of boatmanship, dinghy and canoe sailing in their most extreme forms included. A 40ft *ekdar hora* in a strong monsoon breeze with her big sail set will need all her crew of four or five out on the balance boards, including the helmsman. He must not only steer the boat with lines which may be as much as 20ft long from a yoke on the rudder head, but he must also move constantly and with great sensitivity up and down his balance board as he does so, and at the same time direct the movements of four other men on the boards (page 124).

An *ekdar hora*'s fishing is usually completed in six to eight hours. It is an interesting form of seafaring. For all these hours the crew perch on their spray-soaked frame of timbers, one or more of them always out on the balance boards. There are no cooking facilities and no shelter, no room to lie down and when the men are not performing the unending balancing feat of sailing they are sweating at the oars or hauling nets or lines. These *horas* use lines with 100-150 hooks, gill nets and seine nets.

There is a variation of the *ekdar hora* which is used on the surf-beaten coast west of Karachi. She has a curved stem and sternpost, quite different in shape from those of the rest of the boats in the *hora* group, and a movable rudder which extends a little below the keel and hangs with ordinary gudgeons and pintles, so that it can be removed for beaching. Westwards of Karachi, along the coasts of Las Bela and Makran, these boats are often brought ashore through heavy surf and they are perhaps more strongly constructed than the other types of *hora*. As might be expected, this type of *hora* does not appear ever to be fitted with an outrigger, though balance boards are used with the single small sail. I once spent a week in a hut above the low cliffs of the desert

Page 159 (*above*) The decorated front end of a *bohatja*, and her crew; (*below*) a *bohatja* under construction

Page 160 (*above*) These boats
pulled with heavy sweeps, fitted w
jackstays onto which the crews h
for the 6in sweep is impossible
grasp; (*left*) an Indus punt at Suk

coast west of Karachi. The period was the time of the south-west monsoon and the seas were high with a heavy surf pounding away at the base of the soft sandstone cliffs. Every day a *hora* of the beach boat type was rowed across the bay, regardless of the seas and the wind which took the tops off them, by a crew intent, presumably, upon visiting fish traps.

As Karachi grew and grew, so did the demand of its inhabitants for fish. As the town grew, so did the *horas*. The building began of larger, all plank built reproductions of extended dugouts. This was an extremely important step forward because it freed the men who were used to working with this type of craft from the conventional forms and relative dimensions imposed by a dugout base. At first of course the plank built boats were narrow and deep, like their forbears, and they had outriggers or balance boards or both. But before long, as the local boatbuilders gained confidence, they started to build boats that were much bigger than anything based on a dugout could have been, and far more seaworthy. Outriggers began to disappear, and even the balance board became, as on the small *bheddis*, a moveable fitting, instead of a permanent part of the boat. So *horas* began to be built which could sail with equal efficiency on either tack.

As time went on and these larger *horas* proved themselves successful as fish catching units and consequently as money earners, the local boatbuilders became more enterprising. Greater stability could be obtained by filling out the midships section, and giving rising floors, a deeper keel and a more gentle turn of bilge, giving to the long narrow *hora* something like the sections traditional in the *bheddi*. So the village boatbuilders brought into existence, comparatively recently it seems, a new type of *hora*, beamier, deeper, and altogether more seaworthy than its predecessors. The new type seems to have found its ultimate to date in a sea-going ship 60ft or more long, 6ft deep and 12ft in the beam.

She needs neither outrigger nor balance boards, but she does carry fixed rock ballast and moveable ballast in the form of sandbags on deck. She can, of course, sail without difficulty on either tack, but I have never seen any kind of *hora* go about without being rowed round—the consequence of the long straight keel. She is steered with a tiller, which is fixed at an angle pointing downward from the high rudder head. She has at both bow and stern two stanchions connected by a cross bar on which the long yard rests when the *hora* is not sailing. Her rudder, like those of the smallest ordinary *horas*, is secured to the sternpost with rope lashings.

These great *horas* are still open boats without a continuous deck. Their crews approach seafaring in much the same way as the old inshore fishermen of Britain used to do—those men who, less than 100 years ago, used to go out for days on end in their great open luggers, not so very different in size (in the case of some of the Scots luggers) from the largest *horas*. But the big *horas* catch sharks, and stingray, and swordfish, instead of herring and cod. They catch these big fish with lines, but the sardines and shrimps which they bring home at other seasons are caught with gill nets and seines (page 141). The big *horas* cost much more, in relation to the resources of the fishermen, than the boats of British sailing fishermen did. At the time we did our study of them, in the mid nineteen fifties, a 67ft *hora* cost nearly £1,500 to build.

The building of one of these long open sailing boats begins with the laying of a keel along the top of a series of short posts driven into the ground until they project 18in-2ft above the surface. The keel, even of a big *hora*, is usually in one piece. A curved forefoot with a straight stem piece above and a straight sternpost are secured to this keel by a rather flimsy joint. Often they are simply spiked to the top of the keel. This point of weakness in construction was picked out by one of the commentators on the Food and Agriculture Organisation Report on the *horas*. Mr Arthur Swinfield, an Australian naval architect, said that the most obvious weakness in construction were the stem and sternpost joints to the keel, the length of scarph being inadequate in both cases, and he wondered whether undue leakage did not occur at these points as the *horas* began to age. He suggested, by way of improvement, the adoption of the 'anchor stock' method of joining, because this kind of join is inexpensive and easy to make. At the same time he pointed out that the angle at which the stem and sternpost of the *horas* are set is such as to make the planking of the ends as simple as possible. This aspect of their design has developed naturally, through the inherited experience of their builders.

After the keel and the stem and sternpost have been erected a few floor moulds are sometimes put across the keel and the garboard strakes are fitted. They are fastened to the keel with galvanised iron spikes driven through the side of the plank and out at the lower edge. Slots are cut out in advance to take these spikes and set them at the right angle to the plank face and edge. When the garboard strakes have been fitted, the rest of the thin shell of the planking is built up. The planks are joined to one another, edge to edge, with galvanised iron pegs or pins of about $\frac{3}{16}$in diameter. Before the planks are fitted holes are drilled out in both edges, down into the plank for as much as 2in. The iron pegs are hammered down into the upper holes of the lower plank, already in position on the growing hull, and the upper plank is pressed down over them.

Timber is hard to get in the treeless neighbourhood of Karachi, and most of the materials from which the *horas* are built have travelled hundreds, if not a thousand or more, miles before they reach the boatbuilders on the beaches of Ibrahim Hyderi. Much of the wood for the planks and framing comes from Burma and Malaya. So every piece of wood is valuable and partly owing to this, and partly because the local boatbuilders apparently find the planking at the turn of the bilge especially difficult, the underwater parts of the *horas* are often built up jigsaw fashion out of comparatively short runs of available planking. Indeed, so difficult do they find it to handle the planking of the lower part of the hull, given this traditional method of building and the particular shape of the *hora*'s hull, that the builders frequently leave the turn of the bilge unfinished until the rest of the hull has been planked up.

In the meanwhile the gaping fabric is held together with short lengths of firewood tacked in place here and there as may be required. Similar short lengths are used at the stem and sternposts to hold the ends of each plank as it is fitted. But, apart from the use of a few temporary floor chocks, which, from their battered appearance seem to determine the underwater shapes of many *horas*, and an occasional futtock mould, no moulds are used, and the finished planking is a hollow, flimsy shell, which the frames are cut to fit and into which they are inserted (page 141).

The *horas* as they are planked up require very few struts and braces to support them and the long easy curve of the thin planks require little shoring and clamping. In this way they present a contrast to the boats of the Brahmaputra, with a forest of struts and braces around them to maintain their complicated shape before they are framed up. A *hora* almost fully planked, but not framed, needs only a few poles under her bilge to keep her upright and no shoring to keep her in shape at all. Her shape is essentially an easy one to construct, despite the builders' hesitancy over the bilges, with some of the upper seams parallel for much of their run, and the plank ends at easy angles. *Horas* can, in consequence, be quickly built and, despite their relatively high cost they are still a good deal cheaper than *bheddis.* In the mid-1950s I counted as many as fifteen, of lengths from 15-55ft, under construction at the same time on the beaches of Ibrahim Hyderi.

When the shell of planking is complete, or sometimes when it is only two-thirds or three-quarters complete, the *hora* is framed up. Soft iron rods are bent to fit the inside of the planking and used as moulds to convey the shapes of the frame timbers. The number of frames a *hora* will have depends, within certain limits, on the amount of money her future owner can afford to spend I have seen *horas* of the same size and apparent age, one with twice as many frames as the other. The frames are sawn, and fastened with galvanised iron spikes, driven through planking and frame and clenched over inside. They are usually laid alternately, full frames with floors, and half, or false, frames which do not touch the keel. Framing seems usually to start amidships, and the builders work forward and aft. This is presumably because the weight of the frames in the ends would be likely to distort the planking shell if framing started at bow or stern. Usually there is one riser each side on which rest numerous massive thwarts. In addition to these thwarts, one or two extra large beams are fitted in the large *horas* and iron straps are used as well as wooden knees. On the longest craft two or three extra beams are fitted at gunwhale level.

Whatever the size of the *hora*, she is fitted with very short permanent decks at the ends, while the larger craft have temporary decks laid on the thwarts. Big *horas* have an icebox and galvanised iron fresh water tanks. In the final stage of building the *hora* is caulked with cotton, a local product from the cotton fields up the Indus. It is difficult to tell how much of the *hora*'s characteristic smell comes from the fragments of former catches that tend to lie in the bilges and how much from the shiny fish oil covering of the hull.

According to the fishermen, early *horas* were fastened with wooden pins between the planks and treenails instead of spikes for all the frames and to secure the planks to the frames. I never saw a boat built this way, but there was supposed to be one still in commission in 1952 at Ibrahim Hyderi. It is perhaps of psychological, if not directly of technical, interest that she was spoken of as being a fast, seaworthy craft. This method of fastening perhaps suggests influences on the development of the *hora* from yet another source, because the planking of many of the boats of the Indus is joined, edge to edge, with wooden pins, but these pins are fitted in a manner quite different from the fitting of the iron pins in the horas today. (See pages 177 and 179.)

The basic sail of a *hora*, whatever her size, is a settee with a very short, really vestigial, luff (page 124). Sails on the whole tend to be well shaped and well cut. As with the *bheddis* they are cut from locally made handwoven cloth, or for the light weather sails, from cotton drill. Even the smallest of the plank-extended dugouts sometimes has provision for a mizzen mast, which is stepped during the period of light variable winds from October to March. In small *horas* the mainmast is sometimes stepped off centre, in which case it is always on the outrigger side, where the sail usually works. Thus an ideal pursued by all fishermen who work with small sailing craft is achieved and the sail is kept out of the boat.

A smart *hora* with two shapely settees set, cutting along through the deep blue winter sea, before a smart breeze, is a very lovely sight. At this season of the year larger *horas* set jibs from temporary bowsprits and triangular topsails above their lateen yards. I once saw a small *hora* inside Karachi harbour with two settee sails of the same size set 'goosewinged' from her mainmast. During the calm weather sails are frequently wetted with water thrown on them from the baler to bring the boats back to harbour more quickly on the evening breeze.

During the period of fresh to strong west to south-west winds which lasts from April to September, *horas* use a single sail, usually of smaller dimensions than that set from the mainmast in the cold weather, and often showing signs, by patches and renewals, that it is an old sail which has been subjected to hard wear. Even small *horas* of the *ekdar* type fish far off shore until well into the monsoon season. I have myself seen an outrigger and balance board *hora* out of sight of land as late as 9 May. But during the relatively heavy winds of June, July and August many *horas* are laid up, or confine their fishing activities to Karachi harbour, or to the creeks of the Indus.

Many large *horas* have pleasing traditional designs painted on bow and stern. These are carefully painted and kept fresh. Vestigial oculi appear, sometimes in the form of a crescent and star, sometimes of a star alone. Many of the boats are named and bear their names on bow and quarters. The downwards sloping tillers are heavily decorated with white and blue paint. When the fish oil anti-fouling is being renewed it is smeared on with the palm of the hand dipped in the preparation in tin or enamel bowls. The crews sing at this kind of work, and even stop occasionally to dance and skylark, especially if they have noticed that someone is watching them.

Small *horas* fishing inshore in the cold calm weather often do so in fleets, taking in sails and unstepping their masts as well when they are on fish. These small fleets of *horas* sometimes follow the birds that feed on fish running near the surface, fish driven so close to the air by other fish preying upon them, so that the delicate, water spider-like *ekdar horas* have the appearance, constantly setting and taking in sail, of opening their own wings and feeding off the same fish as do the birds. The waters off Karachi are very rich in sea life. The shoals of small fry are sometimes so thick that they pitter patter along the sides of the boat as she sails quietly along. When racing a 14ft dinghy I have more than once been disconcerted by a fish jumping into the hard-driven boat.

There are two types of models of *horas* to be bought around Karachi. Rough, but accurate, models are made at Ibrahim Hyderi and sailed on the creek by the local children. Better finished, but less accurate, models are made on the islands in Karachi harbour and hawked at higher prices in the town and on the beaches. Both types sail well. On demand the model makers can produce representations of other local craft, and I have a pleasing model of a *bheddi* which is accurate in most respects.

Eight

THE MOTHER RIVER

Frontiers are often an anti-climax, less impressive, and less indicative of change, than the natural boundaries far inside them. But the frontier of Afghanistan and Pakistan at Torkam at the north-western end of the Khyber Pass is not one of these disappointing places. Here the very air changes, because a convenient spring has been put to good use to irrigate the groves of trees on the Pakistan side of the border, and the cool dampness of the trees, and of grass, and the smell of flowers, greets the traveller down from the arid plateau of central Asia. Immaculately turned out scouts of the Khyber Rifles man the frontier. The signboards are provided with an English translation (because English is one of the official languages of Pakistan). The contrast with the dry impoverished uplands of Afghanistan is complete.

The road which winds and twists its way through the Khyber Pass is a great engineering achievement, the railway over and under which the road finds its way many times even more so. In a world so many of whose wonders are currently overrated, the Khyber never disappoints.

There is one point on the eastern side of the Khyber where, as you descend, the valley beneath is suddenly revealed. There is the dry torrent bed at the centre of the Pass, and, layer after layer, the road coils down the mountains like a carelessly thrown hawser on a ship's deck. Beyond, is the shallow V of the eastern mouth of the Pass, and 2,000ft below, a green fertile plain dotted with villages. This, you might feel, is how the Aryans, and Alexander's men, and the Afghan conquerors, and Barbur, the first Great Moghul, and many more, must have looked down upon

India and seen the hot rich plains, and given thanks to their various gods before they went down to them, most in their time to conquer, to grow rich, rule, and be slowly devitalised in their succeeding generations by the awful heat of the Indian summers.

In fact the plain is the lovely Peshawar Valley, a green saucer in the central Asian highland. The geographical sub-continent of India and the plain begins at the Indus River, 60 miles further on and out of sight. And most of the conquerors came by other routes to the north or far to the south of the Khyber.

These northern parts of the province of West Pakistan, comprising the Peshawar Valley, the three little states of Dir, Swat and Chitral, and the Malakand and Khyber Agencies, make up between them one of the most beautiful and varied stretches of country in Asia, if not in the world. It is a country of green fertile, well irrigated valleys, mountains, some snow covered for much of the year, and of rivers. These rivers, the Indus, the Kabul, the Swat and the Kurram run fast and clear among the rocks of the mountains like moorland streams in Britain. Where they break out of the mountains on to the plains they flow through deep steep sided valleys and gorges and here some of them have been harnessed for irrigation and hydro-electric schemes.

In the plains the rivers flow deep and slow. They give life through the irrigation canals which run from them to thousands upon thousands of people. They turn a desert into a moist green land. As navigable rivers always do they form an economical means of transport. Their deep beds are filled with boulders and shingle brought down from the mountains by past summer floods, and boulders and shingle, dredged up, make the foundations of roads and buildings, training walls for the rivers themselves, and ramparts for walled villages. In the swift flowing mountain streams there are mahseer, trout, and sundry other local kinds of fish to be caught and eaten. Everywhere in the plains and in the hills the rivers form a barrier which must be crossed to go from village to village. There are few bridges, and these many miles apart, so where the rivers cannot be waded there must be ferries. Some of such bridges as there are are boat bridges, made up of from fifteen or twenty flat-bottomed craft moored side by side across the stream with a roadway and often sidewalks and safety rails built over them.

For all these purposes boats are needed in this part of central Asia. There are in consequence boat builders in the Peshawar Valley and the art of handling oar and paddle, of handling timber and inflated skin rafts, in the broken waters of mountain torrents, is highly developed. There are hundreds of men who earn their livings in boats and watermanship is a developed and widespread profession, though the Arabian Sea and the fishing boats of Karachi are 1,000 miles away.

The Kabul River comes out of the Khyber hills through the magnificent valley at Warsak, about 20 miles west from Peshawar. Here the Canadian Government has helped Pakistan to build a major hydro-electric and irrigation project which has greatly changed this part of the Peshawar Valley, for much of the area under the hills was desert, despite the rivers which flow through it. The Swat River, which drains the lovely valley of this tiny state in the hills north of the Malakand Pass, breaks down on to the plain of the Peshawar Valley at Abezai Fort, fifteen miles to the north. Once well into the Peshawar Valley the great Kabul River divides itself into three branches which, flowing apart from one another, irrigate and provide communications for quite a lot of the western part of the valley before, after about 20 miles, they join together again and the Swat River joins them too. The combined rivers flow down to the army centre of Nowshera in the middle of the valley, and on and through a break in the eastern edge of the saucer into the great Indus opposite the magnificent old Moghul fort at Attock, above the Indus Gorge, twenty miles further east. Thus the Peshawar Valley is well served with navigable waterways.

It is on these rivers, just to the north of the fascinating old city of Peshawar itself, that the biggest boats of these tributaries of the mother river, the Indus, earn a living for their owners and crews. These boats are about 40ft long, pointed at either end, with flat floors and hard chines. The stem is slightly curved, the stern post broader and raking, faintly reminiscent of the transom of a banks dory. The flat, keel-less bottom has a slight rocker, rising at either end, so that the bottom of the boat at bow and stern is above the water when she is not loaded. They are open for most of their length, but they have short fore and after decks. On these decks the steersmen and the oarsmen stand. The boats are steered with a single large oar working over the stern, most often on the starboard side—the opposite to what is considered to be the right and proper place for steering oars in far away East Pakistan. They are rowed with two oars worked from the foredeck. The oars pull on great single thole pins, cut with regularly spaced notches one above the other, so that the oars can be secured to them by lashings placed at any one of several fixed heights above the gunwhale.

The slightly convex stem is decorated with copper or brass strips, nailed on in a conventional regular pattern, and with a polished wooden knob as an ornament at the stem head. The boats are decorated in other ways as well. Pattern strips are cut into the wood at the 'breaks' of the after deck and the foredeck. Strips of fancily cut brass are nailed along the sheer, which, in all the larger boats, is gracefully curved. The great single thole pins, 3ft high and polished with the working of sweeps and lashings in long miles of steady pulling up and down the big rivers, are often carved and shaped into swans' necks, or into shapes like cobras about to strike. The true oculus does not exist, but something like an eye design often appears. This might be expected, because these boats of the tributaries of the mother Indus are roughly in the middle of the general area of distribution of this device, which stretches from the Atlantic coast of Europe to China. On the boats of the Peshawar Valley it takes the form of a conventionalised circular flower pattern which can be on either bows or stern, and sometimes appears on both. This flower pattern is often cut out of sheet brass.

Small passenger boats, 20 or 30ft long, called *makkuh* in the local dialect, are built on the same lines as the river cargo boats, but instead of the steering oar they have very broad rudders, fixed with a light wooden frame to the broad stern post, and they steer with a tiller. I once came across half a dozen of these little boats, lying at the foot of the broad steps, covered at that time with flood carried sand, which lead down to the river below Attock Fort. New boats, bright, lying awaiting a buyer, they looked splendid on the green river in the bright sun. *Makkuh* are to be found everywhere. They are private boats, watermen's boats and ferryboats on deep streams.

There is another type of cargo boat altogether, a very shallow little craft with pointed ends, which is also used for ferry work but more often for rock and shingle dredging (page 142). And there are the bridge boats, clumsily constructed, high sided, long and narrow, which lie side by side, bobbing gently to the weight of the traffic, the hawsers which secure them groaning to the pressure of the stream.

It was a man working at the repair of a bridge boat, hauled out on the river bank to have new planks put in her, who explained to me one day the processes by which all these boats are built.

He said he was the head of his family, a family of 'boat carpenters'. He was a bearded old gentleman. He spoke Pushtu, the language of the Pathans of the hills around the Peshawar Valley, and through an interpreter he explained to me the simple methods of boatbuilding as he knew them.

First the floor timbers are laid out upside down on a stretch of flat river bank. At either end of the boat-to-be the timbers are small, perhaps 6in deep. Amidships half a dozen timbers may be twice as thick. The keel, a plank of timber 3in thick, is then nailed over the middles of the floor timbers and then, working outwards from the keel plank, the progressively shorter planks of the bottom, each 2in thick, are nailed on and cut to shape at both ends. Peshawar Valley river boats have bottoms planked fore and aft and not cross planked, athwartships. In American terminology they are planked dory style, rather than Chesapeake Bay style. The planks of the bottom are laid flat, edge to edge, without rabbetting, and a caulking of local cotton is driven in between them.

Then the whole bottom of the boat is turned over, and the centre part held down with weights, lumps of rock, while the bow and stern are forced up with poles used as levers to give a slightly increased rocker to the keel. Then the stem and sternpost are fitted; the frames, quite straight with no attempt at any kind of shaping, are added; then the beamshelf and the deck beams, so that at its next stage of construction the boat is an angular skeleton built up on the finished bottom. Last of all she is planked up and the fore and aft decks are laid.

This whole process, the master builder said, took him and his few assistants about twelve days for a cargo boat of normal larger size. Between them, his family had built forty-four boats in the previous year. It was not at all a difficult job. There was no real shipwrighting to be done. Indeed, in all the boats I was able to examine, all the joints between the side frames and the floors, and between the frames and the deck beams were made with cast iron bars and angle irons; there were no scarphs or timber joints.

Despite this apparent weakness the boats wear well, even in the hard trade of stone dredging. The shallow-sided, shallow-draft craft which do this work have a crew of three or four men, and a blanket of straw packed into them to protect the bottom and the sides. They are rowed to a place where the river runs clear, fast and shallow over a bed of small, smooth, water rounded boulders. They are kept afloat—just off the bank—by one man, while the rest, jumping knee or waist deep into the water, proceed to grub up small boulders and big pebbles and throw them into her as fast as they can. While this is going on she inevitably bumps a good deal, and sometimes goes aground in the fast running stream. There are frequent pauses in the work for vigorous baling, partly because a lot of water finds its way on board with the stones. When she is so full she will only just float the boat is rowed or towed from the bank, or drifts with the current to the intended landing place—where stone is collected and broken for the roads, or a site where training walls of loose boulders in steel mesh bags are being built on the riverside. Here the stones are thrown out one by one by hand and the slightly hollow note they make in falling one upon the other, heard over the fields of growing sugar cane, is one of the most characteristic sounds of the winter at the riverside. The only business I know of in Britain to compare with this stone dredging and carrying is the business of collecting sand and gravel from the tidal banks in the Taw and Torridge estuary which used to be carried on in sailing barges from Appledore in North Devon.

I have never seen a boat under sail on these rivers of the north of Pakistan, but craft of similar shape down on the Indus further to the south have tall lateen sails. In the Peshawar Valley the smaller boats, or the big boats when they are light, without cargo, are towed by one man walking on the bank. He does not carry a decorated bamboo and a stirrup, like a Bengal boatman, but has the line around his waist and his hands free. Just in front of the boat the line divides, one part goes to the stem head, one to the stern. Often a short forked branch is stepped at the after end of the foredeck, over which the part of the towing line which goes to the stern is led. It can be seen clearly on page 142. In this way the tendency of the line to pull the boat's stern into the shore is reduced to a minimum. Another man, or a boy, who remains on board, tends the lashed steering paddle and, with another paddle or a pole, keeps the boat away from the shallows.

When a census was taken about 30 years ago there were about 3,000 watermen at work in the Peshawar Valley. Some of them run the numerous ferries—some of these are free to passengers. The boatman lives on food and goods provided for him by neighbouring villages whose inhabitants are dependent on him to get from one patch of cultivation to another. Many boatmen spend all their time looking after boatbridges. This is skilled, exacting never ending work, for the rivers rise and fall constantly all year through. Melting snows, heavy showers, droughts, the pattern of cultivation, the working of irrigation canals and hydro-electric schemes, high winds and the light frosts of winter, all mean that almost daily adjustments have to be made to the complicated structure of a boat bridge. I was told at one bridge of nineteen boats that eight skilled men were constantly employed on it. Where there are boatbridges the cargo boat's range is usually limited to the stretches of water between them and the wheat, sugar cane, *gur*, as the sugar made in the villages is called, hay, stone and straw they carry must be trans-shipped if it is to go further.

Before these Indus tributaries break down the gorges on to the plains they are narrow foaming streams in rocky beds, flowing through mountain valleys of great beauty. Such streams are not suitable for carrying goods, rare though roads are. But goods have to be carried across the streams, and passengers too must be ferried over regularly in many places. There are fish in these streams and all food is precious in the upland valleys.

These rivers are too shallow, and the banks, boulder beds covered at the time of the summer floods, too rough for ordinary timber built craft. Fishing is seasonal, and a part time occupation for peasant farmers and workers. It does not justify capital investment in boats and gear, even if those who live partly by fishing had any money or resources to spare from the grim business of keeping alive at all. For both fishing and ferrying, therefore, a very light craft floating on the surface of the water, cheap and highly portable is required. And the answer to that problem is that ancient device, the raft made of a frame lashed over inflated animal skins.

These rafts are usually made of bullock skins, which are comparatively cheap and easily available. A ferry raft able to carry a dozen people can be made out of six skins with a light frame of poles lashed over them (page 142). She (if you can use the term for a raft of this kind) is pulled by oars (with heart shaped blades lashed on to rough poles in place of the oval shaped boards which make the blades of the valley boats' oars). She can be worked across a torrent (and willy nilly downstream for many times as far as the stream is wide) by a boy who must plod back up the bank dragging the raft behind him on the end of a line to a point upstream of his starting point before loading up again with passengers. I remember an afternoon spent making several such trips. It was fatal to step on the skins instead of the frame, your feet immediately went down into the icy melted snow water and you were in danger of going down altogether. As the raft made each crossing it spun around several times, despite the skill with which its boy pilot handled it. It rocked alarmingly all the time we were on it. But it was perfectly safe as long as the boy did not run it hard into jagged rocks and the people of the upland valley who used it every day did so without worrying. It was really a crude form of a modern inflatable rubber raft or yacht's tender.

Much more hazardous is the type of raft used by the seasonal fishermen. They take two local bedsteads, each a frame of wood covered with a netting of string and equipped with four legs of wood turned on a miniature lathe. Three poles are lashed across these bedsteads to hold them together and then they are turned upside down and four inflated bullock skins tied loosely underneath. The result is an unstable raft, which is equipped with a long pole and no other means of propulsion. It is held in the rushing streams by a rope from either bank, a man on each bank in charge of each end. It has a crew of two men, each equipped with a kind of simple trawl net. The raft is worked backwards and forwards across the stream by pulling the two lines alternately, and then it is allowed to drift downstream a little, and across again, and so on, backwards and forwards, covering the river.

Single, inflated skins are used to support swimmers crossing rivers all over this area. Their use makes it possible to swim in shallow water in rocky streams without danger. Another kind of raft, the timber raft of logs from upland forests comes drifting down the Indus in the autumn and winter. They come from the district called Hazara, down through the great gorge below the bridge at Attock. They are steered with paddles over the stern by lonely watermen who handle them with great skill through the rapids of the low winter river. If these men fall off the raft, which they probably own themselves and hope to sell downstream, nobody ever knows. They just set out, an impoverished waterman owning no more than his raft and what he stands up in, and never return. The timber, scraped and bruised, lodges in some lonely cleft in the rocks, or is picked up by some lucky villager downstream and put to good purpose.

Sukkur is an old, hot, city standing on the west bank of the Indus about 300 miles up its course from the sea. Here the river is broad and deep and, though so much of its water has been taken further upstream for irrigation, irrigation which literally gives life to millions of people, still its current flows swift and strong. At Sukkur is one of the great irrigation barrages from which the canals take off to produce the green, fertile, countryside on both sides of the river downstream.

The barrage means that Sukkur is at the lowest point of navigation on a long and unimportant section of the river. In consequence, and because it is a big centre of local trade in a relatively populous area, the waterfront at Sukkur is lined with river boats loading and discharging, mostly discharging, cargo brought for hundreds of miles slowly with the current down the mother river. And on the shores of sun baked earth boats are built and repaired.

Some of these boats are just like the big cargo boats of the Peshawar Valley, only larger than the largest of the craft on the Kabul River. But most of them are quite different, and the most common type are among the most surprising cargo vessels in use in the world today. They are called by their crews *bohatja* and *darewal battella.*

These boats are flat bottomed craft with the bottoms literally rolled up at either end. The bottoms are the same width from end to end, but the sides bulge. There is no better way of describing them than to refer to the photographs on page 159.

The lower illustration shows how they are built in a single view. First the two sides are assembled. They are made of planks joined edge to edge with wooden pins driven in holes drilled diagonally across the seams from plank face outside to plank face inside. The vertical columns of cut off pin heads are clearly visible in the photograph. The heads are oval shaped because of the angle at which the pins emerge from the plank face. Behind the completed sides the bottom is being made. A row of floor beams like railway sleepers across the dry mud of the river bank has the planks nailed across it, outside ones first, working inwards. The finished bottom is turned over and the sides nailed to the beam ends. The ends of the bottom are forced up at either end to the shape of the sides, and deck beams, longer than the floors so as to force out the sides in a characteristic bulge, are fixed in position, waterways and fore and aft decks are added to make the strong box-like boat, admirably suited to her environment and purpose, which is to be the great cargo carrier of the Indus.

These boats are pulled with heavy sweeps, fitted with jackstays on to which the crews hold, for the 6in thick sweep is impossible to grasp (page 160). Three or four men can pull at each sweep when necessary. When the boats are working downstream they drift with the current, the sweeps are used to give them steerage way and a couple of boys have strength enough to pull them. Then the boats are steered with an immense sweep and the rudders are lifted in the framework by which they are secured to the curved stern. When the boats are working upstream, against the current, then many more arms are needed to pull the sweeps and the boat is steered with the rudder. Sometimes these great cargo carriers are towed from the river bank, and sometimes they sail under a shallow squaresail, its foot extended with a light boom, or a tall lateen sail.

These Indus river cargo boats are beautifully decorated with strips of shining metal, small mirrors, and carved and turned fittings (page 159). They are the only boats of those I have described, except for the boats of the gypsies of the Eastern Province, which have whole families living on board them as a permanent home, women washing the clothes on the foredeck, babies playing on the portable covers of the open hold. Such people cover thousands of miles of the great river in a year's voyaging. They carry their firewood behind them in a dinghy, a miniature of the boats of the Peshawar Valley. Sometimes when the light cargoes of cotton and straw are piled high over the open hold they have to construct tunnels through it to reach their quarters.

But the most common type of boat of the River Indus is very different both from these great cargo carriers and from the boats of the Peshawar Valley. She is a flat bottomed punt, the ends of which are bent upwards to give her a most graceful sheer. This type of boat is to be seen not only on a great stretch of the Indus itself, all the way from the saltings and creeks of the estuary to the plains of the Punjab, but also among the tall reeds of the marshes 60 miles north-east of Karachi, and on the irrigation canals on either side of the river for hundreds of miles.

The river boatmen call this type of boat a *quantel battella.* As it is quite unlike all the other boats of the Indus and its tributaries (except that like all the rest it is a hard-chine, flat-bottomed, craft and represents part of an approach to boats and boatbuilding completely different from the approach of the boatmen of East Pakistan), it deserves some detailed description.

These Indus punts are very graceful and attractive boats, especially when under sail on the great river, or lying at anchor with the tall lateen yard hoisted, under the walls of the old fort at Sukkar (page 160). They vary in size from the 16ft or so of a canal ferry boat, or a marsh fishing boat, to big cargo carrying vessels with covered living accommodation, 50ft or more long. The way they are built, however, appears always to be much the same.

The bottom of the punt is absolutely flat amidships and the planking of this bottom is bent up at a sharp angle at either end. This bottom planking is made up in one piece in the flat from a hotch-potch of planks of different lengths, some of which have sometimes been taken from old boats which have been broken up. The various bits and pieces of the jigsaw puzzle are joined together edge to edge with wooden dowels driven in holes drilled diagonally across the seams. The process is exactly the same as with the great *bohatja* and has already been described above. As with the *bohatja* the ends of the pins are cut off flush with the plank face so that the outside of the bottom is sprinkled with the oval shapes of the cut off dowel ends. The bottom is shaped, a rectangle for the flat section amidships and slightly tapered at the raised ends. Across the bottom, when it has been assembled, light floor timbers are laid at even spaces, with more substantial timbers where the ends are bent up to make the raised ends of the punt. All these timbers, like the knees described below, are fastened to the floor planks with iron spikes.

Next the shaped side planks are assembled in the same way as the planks of the bottom. Of course, the shape to which they are assembled effectively determines the shape of the whole boat, just where, and how much, the bottom planks suddenly turn up to make the raised ends and the curve of the sheer. To force the bottom planking up to fit the sides, levers are used while the flat midships section is held down with stones. The boatmen say this apparently difficult operation, like the apparently even more difficult rolling up of the ends of the *bohatja*, is simple to those with the skill and takes only two or three men to do it.

The bottom planking is attached to the sides by sawn knees so cut as to give to the sides a slight flare. The floor timbers are not bevelled at the ends to fit this flare, but are cut off square with the edges of the bottom planking, so that their ends do not come into contact with the side planking at all. And, as they are fitted quite separately from the side frames and are not only not joined to them, but do not even touch them, they serve only as a means of holding the patchwork of the bottom planking together, and in no sense as frames. There is no chine beam and the only caulking in the boats I was able to examine in detail was one of mud applied to the outside of the join of the bottom with the sides.

The upward sloping parts of the ends are decked with planks laid fore and aft on beams, the ends of the boat are finished off with bands of planks athwartships, laid across each deck from the ends inwards for about a quarter of its length and nailed across the bottom at the ends for a similar distance. The open section of the boat amidships corresponds with the flat run of the bottom planks. There is a heavier beam where each deck ends and the open section begins. The tops of the knees are covered with a covering board and boards are nailed to them to act as a form of ceiling as far down as the beginning of the curved section of the knee.

The small boats of the canals and marshes, left unpainted, are complete as I have described above. Nothing more is done to them and they are ready for use. When they are working they are usually poled along from the foredeck.

The longer boats which carry cargo on the rivers sometimes have a low wooden frame over the open centre section and there, in a little temporary house of turned wooden poles, laths and bamboo woven mats the crew, who are perhaps a family, live during the weeks or months they are away from their village on the river. To give further protection to the open midships section against spray and river waves these big cargo boats sometimes have a washboard, perhaps 2ft high, along the outer edge of the hull. This washboard is a fixture and it is supported by sawn knees permanently attached to the vessel.

These big craft are steered by very narrow, tall rudders and carved, downwards pointing tillers. The rudders are hung from a massive framework built out from the bottom planking of the raised stern section. They are pulled with long sweeps worked by men standing on the foredeck, pulling against great turned and carved single thole pins to which the great sweeps are secured with ropes. They are sometimes partly sculled with a massive paddle made from a plank nailed and lashed to the end of a pole over the port quarter. When working downstream, as with the other Indus River boats, this paddle may be used for steering and the great rudder hoisted up in its frame. The mast rakes forward and the sail set from it may be a lateen or a settee with a vestigial luff. These big cargo punts are covered with some kind of bright varnish-like substance to protect them and they are decorated with carving, particularly on the planking on the underside of the stern where the planks stretch over the water, and on the rudder head.

Despite their superficial similarity in profile to some of the boats of the Brahmaputra, with high sterns and low bows both raised above the water as the description has shown, the resemblance is really of the slightest and these boats of the Indus are as different from the boats of the Eastern Province in construction and presumably in history and origin as boats possibly could be. As to the great *bohatja* with her rolled up ends, I remember seeing in the Uffizi Gallery in Florence an altar panel of the fifteenth century which shows a fragment of what seems to be a large seagoing vessel, the stern only, and that stern is really quite remarkably like the stern of a *bohatja.* Systematic study of Italian paintings of the period might reveal more information and suggest influences which might have been at work in the Indus valley.

As for the punts, their silhouette bears perhaps some resemblance to that of the boat depicted in one of the two scribings of boats found at Moenjo Daro, the Indus civilisation site which lies on the west side of the river roughly in the centre of the long stretch of the Indus on which these boats are to be found today. Models of carts found at Moenjo Daro are exactly like the bullock carts currently found in the locality; but to suggest that the boats remain likewise little changed is to push back the development of the sophisticated flat-bottomed punt a long, long, way in the history of man's efforts to make a living on the water.

Simple people who have suffered no great upheaval in their society tend to cling to the familiar, if it serves its purpose, even though the results of forty generations of slow thought and experiment and chance lies alongside them at the same wharf. This is particularly true of boatmen, partly because to depart from established practice may mean death by drowning, or worse still, loss of the means to keep alive, but mostly because at most times and most places in the story of man boatmen have been poor, and the poor have no means to bring about change.

As I have watched boatmen at work, and seen how they live, in different parts of the world, the truth of this rather obvious statement has been more and more brought home to me. Whether it be the strictly relative poverty of a 'down east' lobster fisherman in New England or maritime Canada with a ten-year-old 100hp truck engine in his fine forty foot boat, and a ten-year-old car to take him to the wharf from his enjoyment of television in a centrally heated house; or of a Japanese beach fisherman with a small semi-diesel engine in his boat and electric power in his cottage; or the absolute poverty of the *malla* of a Dacca *pallar* sweating for the worst months of the year at his 20ft oar for a few handfuls of rice, slowly starving all his life long and carrying with him as he does so three or four diseases all of which can be fatal; boatmen are among the least privileged members of their societies. But the North American and the Japanese can better themselves. The Pakistani cannot.

Despite increasing outside influences the lives of the boatmen of Pakistan still show what a sail and oar economy was really like. Unless the economy was a rapidly expanding one (as happened at times in the history of North America), it was for most of its members a life without hope. The simplest, cheapest outboard motor which in Britain drives an inflated rubber yacht-tender could revolutionise the life of the owner of a twenty foot passenger and cargo dinghy, give him a standard of living that was above simply remaining alive. He is sustained in the general horror of his situation by his knowledge of God, by the family system which tends, where there is a family, to prevent complete starvation, and because all around him are people in the same situation, and he himself has conceived of nothing else.

Prosperity for the boatman is unattainable, riches impossibly remote. To keep alive and enjoy the passing moment, to keep out of trouble and in employment, these are his highest ambitions. In the history of getting a living on the water this is how most boatmen have lived. This is the gulf between sailing for a living and sailing for pleasure. He who sails for a living ceases only to die.

AUTHOR'S NOTE AND BIBLIOGRAPHY

Like *The Merchant Schooners*, *Boats and Boatmen of Pakistan* is based largely on fieldwork, the recording of observations and of first hand accounts of methods and practices and historical incidents—in this case done in Pakistan during a residence totalling rather more than five years spread over the decade of the 1950s. The greater part of this time was spent in East Pakistan, but we travelled very widely in both provinces of the country, in Afghanistan and in neighbouring states of India. The fieldwork on the boats and the lives of those who depended on them was a leisure occupation in some ways complementary to the professional purpose of my residence in the country. This study of the boats and boatmen, although often carried out in difficult and uncomfortable circumstances, was for what it revealed a most rewarding operation. I do not know of many such detailed studies of groups of boats and the life around them. I hope there will be more in the future, and that they will take more account of the detail of building methods than has sometimes been the case in the past.

The seminal work for this study was a paper written in Tokyo in 1956 from field notes prepared in the period 1950-4 for publication in *The Mariner's Mirror*, the quarterly journal of the Society for Nautical Research. This paper was subsequently reprinted as a pamphlet and published under the title *The Boats of East Pakistan*. The present book was first drafted in Dacca in 1959 and subsequently worked on in Ottawa, Bideford and London, where it was completed 10 years later.

Pakistan is developing, but the life of the eastern province still remains largely sail and oar based. Despite more roads and motor launches the picture of that life given remains generally true. But the life is changing, and there have been great developments in the fishing industry of Karachi so that it has moved away from the relatively simple nineteenth-century-style industry described here. This book therefore provides a portrait in detail of a group of relatively pure sail and oar based economies at the peak of their development. Unlike *The Merchant Schooners*, the world it describes is not yet a 'world we have lost' but we soon shall have lost it and nothing like it has existed in Europe since before the First World War.

There are two main strands in the various evolutions of the plank built boat, shell construction and skeleton construction. The first comprises the process of building up the planks of the boat, joined edge to edge by one means or another, and then inserting the frames, cut to fit the shell of the planks. Thus the shape of the boat is determined at the planking, not the frame stage. Shell constructed boats may in fact have no frames at all. Skeleton construction comprises the process of setting up the shaped frames of the boat first and then wrapping them round with a skin of planks. Thus the shape of the boat is determined by the frames.

In Northern Europe, shell construction is associated generally with planking laid with overlapping edges, lapstrake or clinker fashion, skeleton construction with smooth-skinned boats with the planking laid edge to edge. Most study of the history of the evolution of the boat has been done by North Europeans and North Americans conditioned to these local circumstances, and confusion of thought has followed because there has been a tendency to identify smooth-skinned boats with the skeleton construction. The reader will have noted that of all the boats described in this book only one relatively small group are of skeleton construction though almost all are smooth skinned. I am myself inclined to the view that shell construction has been far more widespread than has sometimes previously been supposed and that skeleton construction—which is far more difficult—is a relatively new invention spreading out from Europe with the expansion since the fifteenth century. But much more research work will have to be done before even tentative conclusions are possible.

Very little indeed has been published about the aspect of the life of Pakistan dealt with in this book. I have already mentioned Hornell's work. His description is incomplete and his lack of opportunity to study the structure of the boats in detail led him into a number of confusions particularly over the matter of shell and skeleton construction. Nevertheless, *Water Transport*, Newton Abbot, 1970, remains an essential introduction to its subject and the description of the Bengal boats is particularly useful. A detailed description of the Karachi fishing boats as they were in the mid-nineteen-fifties, but again paying relatively little attention to construction and building methods, was published in Food and Agriculture Organisation *Report No 403 Report to the Government of Pakistan on the Mechanisation of West Pakistan Fishing Boats*, Rome, 1955.

For the general background of the life in East Pakistan, Nafis Ahmad's *An Economic Geography of East Pakistan*, Oxford, 1958, is invaluable and has an excellent bibliography. *District Gazetteers* covering a number of areas of East Pakistan were published in Calcutta in the early years of this century. They contain a certain amount of local information about the boats and the life around them, some of which has to be used with care.

I know of no published account of any substance about the boats of the Indus and its tributaries.

Of the drawings, figures 1-18 were drawn under my supervision by Cicely Hill. Figures 19-22 have been re-drawn by kind permission of the Food and Agriculture Organisation of the United Nations from Report No 403. All the photographs are my own. The maps are by Donald Cufflin.

I am particularly grateful to the late Harold Underhill for his comments on the penultimate draft of this book. I wish to acknowledge with gratitude the help given to me in doing the fieldwork by Nurul Alam, Lutfur Rahman and Syed Enver Masood, James Blair, Bishop of Dacca, Walter Ravenscroft and Frank and Barbara Lisle-Taylor. Ann Gifford made the index.

London 1970 Basil Greenhill

INDEX

Page numbers in **bold** type indicate illustrations